The Guatemala Reader

Extraordinary Lives and Amazing Stories

Mark D. Walker

In Memory

IN MEMORY OF
Maria E. Martin
Pioneering Latina Public Radio Journalist

IN HONOR AND APPRECIATION OF

Ricardo Rodriquez (Kacalo), my Guatemalan father-in-law
who took our family all over the country on the weekends,
and my mother-in-law, Antonieta, who helped care for our
children in their early years.

PRAISE

Praise for the Guatemala Reader

"Mark Walker's ***The Guatemala Reader*** provides a wonderful excursion through the Land of Eternal Spring that will delight "old hands" and "newbies" to Guatemala alike. It delivers hard truths as well as enchanting insights. As a 50+ year student of all things Guatemalan, I can enthusiastically say the book is a modern-day classic." Bob Graham, Author, ***50-50 at 50***, Founder of the Katalysis Partnership and Namaste Direct.

"... In ***The Guatemala Reader***, the author begins with a truth that all travelers will endorse. There is always one place, one culture, and country, that becomes your personal lodestar. Your sense of the world in its ragged variety is guided by it. For Walker, Guatemala is that country, and the careful intelligence with which he has assembled the collection testifies to his deep understanding of the place and the people who live there. The individual pieces are varied in theme and approach. The evocative illustrations are superb. Even the map is just right, identifying the numerous locales in which Walker has worked, lived, and learned to appreciate the complex cultural reality that is Guatemala. This book is for everyone." Mark Jacobs is the author of ***Stone Cowboy*** and **Silent Light.**

"Mark Walker's ***The Guatemala Reader*** is much more than eye-opening journeys through the history, folklore, politics, art, and literature of Guatemala. It is enriched by personal accounts of in-depth experiences over a lifetime of living and traveling the stunningly diverse and complex cultural, linguistic, and physical landscapes of the country. It is also particularly timely during these challenging times of migrations from Central America to the United States, for it offers an opportunity to build bridges across cultures, paths for understanding and connecting with migrants who, in all their diversity, may at first appear strangely, perhaps threateningly different and monolithic. Yet ***The Guatemala Reader*** offers inspiring escape hatches from misleading, oversimplified stereotypes and opens the possibility for enriching personal and humane engagement. As a former Peace Corps Volunteer, like Mark, I see his book as an important and increasingly relevant and fulfilling contribution to the Third Goal of The Peace Corps: 'To help promote a better understanding of other peoples among Americans,' Bravo Mark!" Joe Lurie, Author ***Perception andDeception-A Mind-Opening Journey Across Cultures***, Emeritus Executive Director, UC Berkeley's International House.

"Mark D. Walker's deep familiarity with Guatemala makes The Guatemala Reader an invaluable resource for anyone who wants to know more about this fascinating but frequently misunderstood country. Since the 1970s, when he arrived in Guatemala as a Peace Corps volunteer, Walker has studied and explored the country while passionately advocating for its indigenous peoples. Blending storytelling with analysis, The Guatemala Reader is brimming with wisdom, insight, and compassion. Mark D. Walker is the ideal guide for those looking for a deeper understanding of the issues confronting Guatemala and Central America." Stephen Benz, Author **Guatemalan Journey,** and **Topographies**, Professor of English Literature, University of New Mexico.

"This is a great collection of essays by Mark Walker, some evocative of a beautiful country, some quivering with hard facts and descriptions, all fully illustrative of what has been happening in Guatemala for the last half-century and more. These are indeed "Extraordinary Lives and Amazing Stories." Walker's connection to Central America goes back over fifty years. He's read widely about Guatemala and followed the internal wars there, the injustices to the indigenous population, and, most recently, the massive waves of emigration. He's been involved through his family and various jobs, and his passion for the county is evident. Whether you know much or little about Guatemala, you'll learn plenty here about the engaging culture and history of this remarkable near-neighbor of ours." John Thorndike, Author *A Hundred Fires in Cuba*, *Another Way Home: A Single Father's Story.*

"To be honest, I agreed to read Mark Walker's *The Guatemala Reader* as a favor to a fellow scribbler, not out of any particular interest in Guatemala. But while I began the book as a favor to Mark, I kept on reading as a favor to myself. I was pulled in by the stories of some fascinating characters—And why do any of us read if it's not for stories?—and by some of the book's universal themes: the personal cross-cultural journeys of Mark, his wife Ligia, and a handful of expatriates; the exploitation and oppression of indigenous people (in this case the Maya) by greedy foreign companies and their implicit governments; the courage of those who oppose injustice; the wisdom and life lessons of the marginalized and the downtrodden." Craig Storti is the author of Why Travel Matters, The Hunt for Mount Everest, and the founder of Communicating Across Cultures.

"...Guatemala's history is not easy to digest. For those interested in understanding what Mark and I were attempting to do in our documentary, *A Guatemala Reader* will offer a wealth of information from a largely Guatemalan point of view; it will include diverse academics, extraordinarily savvy journalists/novelists, indigenous artists, and writers. It will unlock a good portion of the country's beautiful mystery and its tragic history." Hal Rifken, Filmmaker Behind the Strings, Girl Island, Blue Like Me: The Art of Siona Benjamin. (Hal and I worked on a documentary about immigration issues in Guatemala, **"Trouble in the Highlands,"** for three years but could not complete it due to COVID-19).

"The Guatemala Reader by Mark Walker is a "must read" book for those planning to visit Guatemala. It is for visitors who want more than tours to spectacular Maya and Olmec temples to enjoy the unique music of the marimba or marvel at the colorful clothing produced by cottage industry weavers across the country. His book offers readers much to those who seek to better understand what they are seeing and experiencing in this ancient land of many cultures, languages, and customs. **The Guatemala Reader** provides straight-talk about the good and the worrisome in beautiful modern Guatemala. I wish I had had a book like it when I first visited Guatemala 35 years ago! Walker's many years in Guatemala and other Latin American countries give him a perspective most people can only dream about acquiring. His selections for this book include essays from other authors, journalists, and scholars, and all are well-written or translated and are enjoyable reads. The book is organized into four sections; the first is a romp through Maya history, myths, utopian thinking, travel in Guatemala, Maya, folklore, arts, and literature. His selections provide information about Guatemala as seen through the lens of Guatemalan literary and biographical writers. The collection of essays with different perspectives of this wonderful, beautiful, and complex country is excellent. My favorite essay is "The Making of the Kingdom of Mescal, an Adult Fairy Tale."

...His chapter on the Yin and Yang of Travel is fun. His excursions present tantalizing insights that will help visitors understand what they are seeing in a country whose indigenous people cling to their cultural traditions while faced with immense cross-pressures from external organizations of religion, finance, law enforcement, the military, and governance controlled by the elite. His presentation moves quickly and is packed with information on various dimensions of the creative energy that is contemporary Guatemala and is respectful of the Maya people...At the back of the book are useful and easy-to-understand data on population characteristics and how these have changed over the years. Did you know, for example, that the percentage of the Indigenous Maya population has remained steady since 1970, but their religious affiliation, once 95% with the Catholic church, shrank until today, when 40 percent self-identify as Evangelicals?" Earl Vincent de Berge, Poet and Writer *A Finger of an Old Man's Hand: Adventures in Mexico's Baja Wilderness, Allegro to Life, Wind in the Elephant Tree.*

DISCLAIMER

This is a work of nonfiction, meticulously crafted over more than fifty years. The Guatemala Reader is a compilation of essays that delves into the events I have personally tracked and the individuals I have had the privilege to meet. In pursuing authenticity, I have drawn information from various books and cited sources when describing historical periods and facts. However, as this is not a thesis or an academic paper, footnotes have been omitted.

It is important to note that the research and writing of this book have been solely conducted by me, without the use of artificial intelligence. My intellect, passion, and personal experiences have driven the entire process. I firmly believe in the power of human connection and understanding, and I wanted this book to reflect that.

The essays included in The Guatemala Reader were initially published in the Revue Magazine over the past three years. They offer a candid account of my memories and opinions and those of the individuals I have had the privilege to profile.

While I have made every effort to ensure the accuracy of the information presented in this book, I humbly acknowledge that I have been wrong on occasions throughout my lifetime. As you delve into the pages of The Guatemala Reader, you may come across instances where my understanding and recollection have faltered. These moments remind us of our shared humanity and the continuous journey of learning and growth.

Should you have any inquiries or wish to connect with the author, please get in touch with me at mark@millionmilew alker.com or visit millionmilewalker.com.

Acknowledgments:

I sincerely thank Don McCauley of the Free Publicity Group for his exceptional cover design. Clifford Nagle skillfully captured the captivating photo of the Mayan girl on the cover. Fellow Returned Peace Corps Volunteer Jay Schuff took the background photo. Additionally, I would like to thank Zenon Schafer for granting permission to include several illustrations of Nan Cuz's "In the Kingdom of Mescal."

INTRODUCTION

Introduction

For every world traveler, there is a place in one's memory that is a paradise—mysterious, beautiful, and full of alluring secrets. A place where one can return to by closing one's eyes. Guatemala is mine.

My journey began as a Peace Corps volunteer when I met and married a local lady and had three children there. For more than fifty years, I've worked in, and returned to, the Land of the Eternal Spring as a development manager, fundraiser, and tourist.

Over the years, I've met and gotten to know people from all walks of life in Guatemala—from the poorest, humblest Maya farmers in the highlands to wealthy plantation owners, some "Ladinos" (Guatemalans who have replaced traditional garb with European-style clothing and speak Spanish), leaders from innumerable Non-Governmental Groups (NGOs), writers, painters, filmmakers, and professionals of many types. Some are politically conservative, pro-business, some left-leaning, but each one has an appreciation of Guatemala.

Fortunately, I took the time to explore the country and appreciate its complex culture and many spectacular sites such as Antigua, Lake Atitlan, Quetzaltenango (Xela), the coast, Rio Dulce, and the Maya ruins of Tikal encompassed in a jungle with howler monkeys screaming and throwing branches at passing tourists. Many images come to mind when thinking of Guatemala: the volcanoes, high arid mountains of the Piedmont and endless coffee plantations, the South coast with vast fields of sugar cane and pastures for humped Cebu cattle.

The pungent smell of wood fires in the rural highland villages is my most memorable odor, although the earthy, moist smell of the fecund jungles in the Petén has its unique scent. The colorful open marketplaces are filled with a rainbow array of exotic fruits like papaya, *nisperos*, *granadillas*, and plump yellow lemons. The aromas of fresh fruit and those of raw, sometimes aging meat whose stench is often covered by the sweet smell of incense. The sounds are the soft, mellow tone of the *marimba* playing "Guatemala Luna de Xelau" or the piercing oboe-like sound of the double-reeded *chirimía* flute accompanied by a large drum during Holy Week. A religious procession passes with scores of worshippers carrying heavy floats with the Passion of Christ passing over colorful sawdust carpets under a convent arc of Santa Elena in Antigua, built in the 17th century.

Many of these images and smells come together on or by the entrance to the church in Chichicastenango, which combines colorful flowers, fruits and vegetables, and animals dead and alive with the sound of the *marimba* leading up to the entrance of the iconic Santo Tomas Church where chickens are sacrificed while pilgrims enter to worship.

Although Guatemala is best known for its volcanic landscape, fascinating Maya culture, and the colorful colonial city of Antigua, a UNESCO World Heritage Site, it has a history troubled by colonization, military dictatorships, guerrilla conflicts, and interference from that colossus to the north, the United States. The great Maya cities fell into obscurity, and their inhabitants scattered only to develop today's viable Maya communities. This long history helps one appreciate the country's complex makeup and the future direction it might take.

As I learned about the role the United States played in the demise of any semblance of democracy and any level of economic and social equity in Guatemala, I felt more obligated to make up, in my small way, for the damage of my country's misguided policies. I tried to listen to and support local leaders and professionals over the years, which became a driving force in why and where I've traveled and worked during the fifty years since arriving in Guatemala as a volunteer.

I'm sad that Guatemala is still an impoverished country with a painful disparity between the wealthy and the poor. It has one of the highest child mortality rates in the world, especially among the Maya community, which accounts for almost 50% of the population. And yet, it is a place of redemption and inspiration, which is evident in its children and the young people who decide to stay and make a living there.

*The **Guatemala Reader*** brings together sixteen essays, maps, graphs, and photos to celebrate Guatemala, those who impacted the country, and those whose lives were changed after moving there. This story goes beyond the long experience of conflict, racism, and violence so often focused on, especially during the ongoing immigration crisis.

Most of the essays have been published in the *Revue Magazine,* an English-language publication based in Antigua with an expatriate audience throughout Central America and the U.S. The book is not a series of documents from an academic journal, but a collection of essays with different perspectives of this wonderful, beautiful, complex country.

The essays are divided into four sections, starting with "Seeing Guatemala Through Literary and Biographical Prisms." These essays highlight the country's diversity and complexity and why twenty-two Mayan languages beyond Spanish are spoken. "The Making of the Kingdom of Mescal, an Adult Fairy Tale," is a story within a story with an intriguing Maya and German twist. "Gods and Monsters"includes tales told for two thousand years in the Maya area. The following essay concerns Maya writer and anthropologist Victor Montejo and some of his most memorable books. "Allegro to Guatemala" focuses on the impact of one of the many expatriate couples living in Guatemala, and "Uncovering the Art of Francisco Goldman" profiles one of the best-known contemporary Guatemalan writers.

The following four stories are part of my "Yin and Yang of Travel" series, a portal into the world of timeless travel and what can go wrong. It was inspired by Paul Theroux's *The Tao of Travel*. "Traveling in Tandem with a Chapina" chronicles how traveling with my new Guatemalan wife changed how and why I traveled. "Tschiffely's Epic Equestrian Ride" follows the monumental 10,000-mile trek of a thirty-year-old high school headmaster in Argentina. "Traveling Through the Land of the Eternal Spring" details where I traveled in Guatemala and the books I read over the years to learn and appreciate the country even more. My Saddest Pleasures deals with the most challenging donor tours I led throughout the world.

The following six essays make up "Crossing Borders," starting with "The Future of the Peace Corps in Guatemala," which is the story of the fifty-two hundred volunteers who have served there for over sixty years through the eyes of one volunteer who was given just a few days in 2020 to evacuate the country due to COVID-19. "Hugs Not Walls: Reuniting the Children" tells the chilling story of how U.S. government policy resulted in children being taken from their parents during the asylum-seeking process, unable to unite with them. "Trouble in the Highlands" was the basis for a documentary on immigration challenges in Guatemala. "Justice & Responsibility: The Plight of the Immigrants from Central America" reports on the "push" and "pull" factors motivating so many Guatemalans to come north. "Crossing Borders, Building Bridges: A Journalist's Heart in Guatemala" profiles a radio journalist who still lives in Guatemala and has focused on training the next generation of Maya radio journalists over the last twenty years.

The book ends with a historical overview of contemporary Guatemala. I also provided a "Guatemala Fact Sheet," "A Comparative Atlas of Impunity Chart," and a bibliography of all the essays included here, recommended reading, and available resources. This book was written for travelers, scholars, students, and practitioners alike, as it presents the stark realities behind the beautiful facade.

Contents

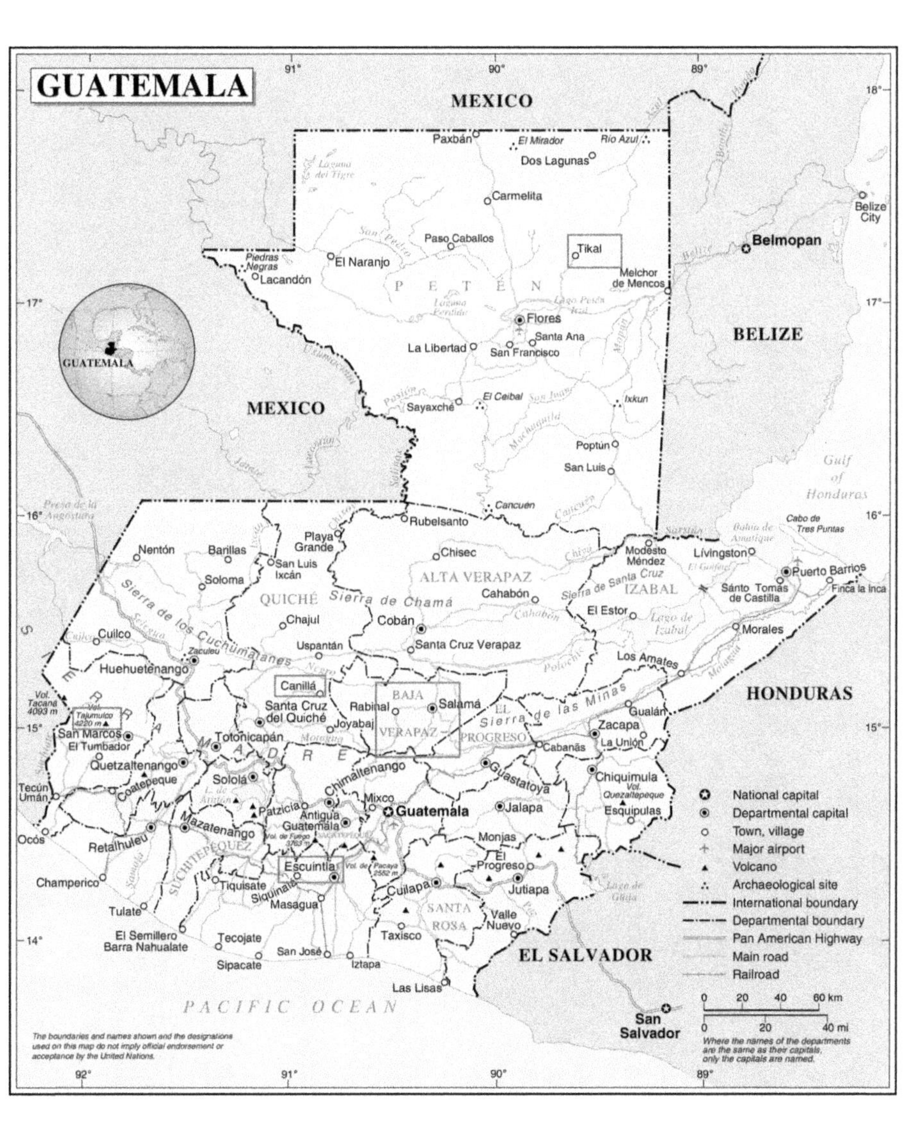

GUATEMALA
MEXICO
91°
90°
89°
18°
Paxbán
El Mirador
Río Azul
Dos Lagunas
Laguna del Tigre
Carmelita
Belize City
San Pedro
Paso Caballos
Tikal
Belmopan
Piedras Negras
El Naranjo
Melchor de Mencos
Lacandón
P E T É N
Belize
17°
Laguna Perdida
Lago Petén Itzá
Flores
BELIZE
Santa Ana
La Libertad
San Francisco
GUATEMALA
El Ceibal
San Juan
Ixkun
MEXICO
Sayaxché
Machaquilá
Poptún
Pasión
San Luis
Gulf of Honduras
Cabo de Tres Puntas
Presa de la Angostura
Cancuén
Cancuén
Bahía de Amatique
16°
Rubelsanto
Sarstún
Livingston
Modesto Méndez
16°
Nentón
Barillas
Chisec
Chixoy
El Golfete
Puerto Barrios
Playa Grande
Santa Cruz
San Luis Ixcán
ALTA VERAPAZ
IZABAL
Finca la Inca
Soloma
Sierra de Santa Cruz
Sánto Tomás de Castilla
Cahabón
QUICHÉ
Sierra de Chamá
Cabañón
Lago de Izabal
Cuilco
Cuilco
Sierra de los Cuchumatanes
Chajul
Cobán
El Estor
Morales
Zaculeu
Uspantán
Santa Cruz Verapaz
Polochic
Huehuetenango
Negro
Los Amates
Motagua
Canillá
BAJA
Salamá
HONDURAS
Vol. Tacaná 4093 m
Santa Cruz del Quiché
Rabinal
Sierra de las Minas
Gualán
Vol. Tajumulco 4220 m
Joyabaj
VERAPAZ
EL
Zacapa
15°
San Marcos
Totonicapán
Motagua
PROGRESO
Cabañas
La Unión
15°
El Tumbador
M
A
D
R
E
Guastatoya
Quetzaltenango
Solalá
Chimaltenango
Chiquimula
Coatepeque
L. de Atitlán
Mixco
Guatemala
Jalapa
Vol. Quezaltepeque
Tecún Umán
Patzicía
Esquipulas
National capital
Antigua Guatemala
Departmental capital
Ocós
Mazatenango
Vol. de Fuego 3763 m
Monjas
Town, village
Retalhuleu
SUCHITEPÉQUEZ
SACATEPÉQUEZ
El Progreso
Major airport
Escuintla
Vol. de Pacaya 2552 m
Volcano
Champerico
Tiquisate
Cuilapa
Jutiapa
Lago de Güija
Archaeological site
Siquinalá
International boundary
Tulate
Masagua
SANTA
Valle Nuevo
Departmental boundary
ROSA
Taxisco
Pan American Highway
El Semillero
Tecojate
Main road
Barra Nahualate
San José
EL SALVADOR
Railroad
Sipacate
Iztapa
0   20   40   60 km
Las Lisas
0   20   40 mi
PACIFIC OCEAN
San Salvador
Where the names of the departments are the same as their capitals, only the capitals are named.
The boundaries and names shown and the designations used on this map do not imply official endorsement or acceptance by the United Nations.
92°
91°
90°
89°

PART I

SEEING GUATEMALA THROUGH LITERARY AND BIOGRAPHICAL PRISMS

"Don't forget the teachings of the ancestors. In their paths, we will find hope for the future." A Maya Elder

Chapter 1

THE MAKING OF "IN THE KINGDOM OF MESCAL: AN INDIAN FAIRY TALE FOR ADULTS"

I discovered this book among items my parents had left. A colorful, mystical figure holding the hand of a small boy dominated the front cover. On the inside cover was an inscription from my wife's Guatemalan/German friends, who gifted the book when they visited my parents in Evergreen, Colorado, at Christmastime in 1978. My wife's friends knew the author, although his name was not listed anywhere. The book merely cited the publisher, Galleria Panajachel,

Lake Atitlán, Guatemala; the year of publication, 1977; and the German printer. Enchanted by the tale, I researched and soon identified the author as Georg Schafer, a German painter and poet, and the illustrator was Schafer's Guatemalan-born wife, Nan Cuz.

Although the story begins with "Once upon a time," it is anything but traditional. The book is based on Guatemalan art and music collected by Schafer and the early memories of Nan Cuz, born to a Maya woman. It is also strongly influenced by the psychedelic drug culture of the time.

To my surprise, the story was inspired by another adult fairy tale, **The Little Prince**, by Antoine de Saint-Exupéry, a poetic adventure with the author's watercolor illustrations.

Unlike the little prince, who leaves his home with the help of a flock of migrating birds, the Indian boy, Blackhair, the young seeker at the heart of *In the Kingdom of Mescal*, uses a magic potion as the medium for transportation of the mind. Just as the prince visits other planets, each revealing a new story, Blackhair embarks on a journey of revelation and gains a greater understanding of himself and the world around him.

Blackhair desires to see beyond the surface of the world and gets his wish when a local medicine man gives him a potion that transports him to a vast forest lit by a full moon. The medicine man promises to take him to the Kingdom of Mescal, where all his queries will be answered. That night, Blackhair does as the medicine man advised, and as the landscape around him begins to dance, his fears dissolve, his feet grow massively significant, and he vomits up a talking serpent. The snake identifies itself as Time and starts the boy on his quest.

That quest involves a trip through the sky inside a raindrop, a malevolent emperor who rides a donkey with one hundred legs, trees that bow and talk, a palace with one thousand doors, and the excellent Lord of Mescal, who takes Blackhair on an interplanetary voyage before imparting some timeless wisdom. Along the way, Blackhair is stopped by a sharp-toothed, feathered giant who warns him that the journey through the kingdom of thoughts will be dangerous. The giant gives the boy a golden robe and says his disloyal servants will try to lead him astray, but the Kingdom of Mescal will open before him if he escapes them. Blackhair continues his journey, encountering a series of perils, including a hissing, many-headed reptile. Blackhair survives, and the Lord of Mescal grants him the key to men's hearts, lovingkindness, and the clarity of mind to help them find the right way. When he returns, Blackhair possesses nothing, but his people come to regard him as the richest of men and a great seer. Schafer's rendering of this supernatural tale, told in simple, unadorned language, makes little distinction between fantasy and reality. But it is Cuz's colorful full-page illustrations, reminiscent of Maya art and weaving, that bring these stories to life.

Besides being a writer, Schafer, who went by the name Oma Ziegenfuss, was an artist, visionary, mystic, philosopher, and romanticist. During World War II, he distributed pamphlets for the Danish resistance, but was captured by the Gestapo and sentenced to death for espionage. Himmler commuted his sentence to fifteen years in prison, which Schafer spent in five concentration camps until the war ended. Around 1950, after working and studying at the Theological College at Fulda, he became a journalist for a newspaper in Hamburg, where he met Irmgard Cuz Heinemann, a photographer for the same newspaper. The couple married in 1952.

Heinemann, known as Nan Cuz (her Q'eqchi' Maya family name), was born in 1927 in the village of Secoyocte, in the municipality of Senahú in Alta Verapaz, Guatemala, to a Q'eqchi' mother and a German father, a wealthy coffee plantation owner. Nan was brought up under her grandmother's supervision. Spanish was prohibited in the household of eight children, who spoke only their native Q'eqchi'. The Maya family structure is strictly matriarchal, and I couldn't find a reference to Nan's grandfather in my research, making her grandmother and mother the dominant influences in her upbringing.

The family lived in the north-central part of Guatemala in a lush tropical forest that receives up to nine feet of rain per year. The diversity of plant and animal life is impressive. There are innumerable insects and colorful birds, including the quetzal, with its spectacular emerald green and red plumage, and many different predators, such as jaguars and cougars. Their religion is based on a symbiosis with Roman Catholicism. Their view of the earth and the afterlife is reflected in ceremonial sites located in caves like the one I visited when leading a donor tour to the area. The cave got darker as I climbed down until I reached a place of candles and copal, a tree sap used as incense. These caves are often described as entries into the watery Maya underworld. Life begins and ends in the middle zones between this world and the underworld, associating caves with life and death.

Even at an early age, Nan carried images of this mystical, green world, and as an adult, she would refer to her "mysterious talks with the rainforest" and "visions" she'd had while walking through the cornfields. She also believed that "Mother Earth provides everything, but we treat her badly" and that one must ask Mother Earth's permission to experience a true "feeling of oneness." Her art reflects the deep and eternal connection between the earth, nature, and all living beings. These myths, visions, colors, landscapes, animals, and plants, buried deep in her psyche, emerged in her art and the illustrations of *In the Kingdom of Mescal*.

Nan's village was in the center of a German settlement formed in the 1870s in Alta Vera Paz. It became the primary source of timber and coffee for European markets. By the end of the 19th century, Germans owned seventy-five percent of the land, and a governor reported that peasants were fleeing from the landowners for whom they were forced to work. Nan said that her father, Hermann Heinemann, had "stolen" her mother, Filomena Cuz, from her village. He baptized his daughter with a combination of Germanic names—Irmgard Cuz Heinemann—that no one in the village could pronounce. They called her Nan Cuz.

Life on the German plantations was far from what Nan would have been accustomed to in her village. The "Big House" of one of these plantations would have included innumerable bedrooms, a living room, and a kitchen, with five or more kitchen helpers. It would have had electricity and drinkable water. A group of gardeners would have cut the grass and cultivated the exotic tropical flowers with nothing more than a machete. Hundreds of Maya workers worked on the plantation at any given time, cleaning the coffee plants or harvesting the beans. Then, they processed and dried them on a large patio, cleaning and placing the coffee in large sacks to export to Europe. Some of the growers sent their shirts with the coffee down the Río Dulce, to the Caribbean, and back to Germany, where the coffee would be sold, and the shirts washed, pressed, and returned on the next trans-Atlantic ship returning to Guatemala.

By contrast, a Maya house like Nan's was usually a good hike from the road. It had a thatch-roofed kitchen in the back and a wood-plank dwelling in the front with small, glassless windows, making for a relatively dark space inside. Sometimes up to eight family members would sleep in a small dwelling like this. Many people had a small altar with both Christian symbols like the cross and Maya symbols like an ear of corn, and candles surrounding the entire display. Firewood would be piled up on the front porch. Several coffee and fruit trees, such as bananas, would surround the home. The animals, including chickens and piglets, could be found behind the kitchen, which didn't have a chimney, so the smoke from the fire would slowly drift up and out of the roof. Out in the back was a small round structure with a tiny opening, where one could enter to throw water on heated rocks for a steam bath.

Hermann Heinemann abandoned the family when Nan was young. Still, seven years later, his second wife, who was German, traveled to Guatemala to take Nan to Germany, where she would receive a "good education." Taking the same route as the plantation owners' shirts, Nan hiked down to Panzós, which means "place of the green waters," along the Polochic River and swamps full of alligators and exotic birds. The river would eventually take her to Lake Izabal and down the Rio Dulce, which runs through a thick jungle filled with screeching monkeys and birds.

The Rio Dulce reminded me of Joseph Conrad's classic *Heart of Darkness* scenes, as the river meandered through a dense jungle. Eventually, Nan's boat would arrive at Puerto Barrios in the Caribbean, where she'd board a steamer bound for Europe with her new German mother. One can only imagine how a seven-year-old who spoke only Q'eqchi and had never worn shoes felt when she arrived in the Netherlands in the dead of winter and, eventually, Germany, in the Nazi era. Nan learned German, which her peers respected, although they taunted her for her small size and brown skin, calling her "little monkey."

Nan's mother agreed to her departure only if her daughter would be sent home after her schooling. But World War II broke out, and Nan didn't see her mother again for thirty-seven years. She called her stepmother Mena Cuz, or "Other Mother," and found her very domineering. Her sense of guilt over not seeing her birth mother and losing contact for so long was profound, as reflected in her series of Madonna and Child paintings.

When the war ended, Nan was eighteen. Her father was a professional photographer and taught Nan the craft, although she preferred to paint. In 1950, she met and married Georg Schaefer. In 1971, they left Germany with their two children. They settled in Guatemala, where they created La Galeria de Nan Cuz, which would become Panajachel's social, intellectual, and artistic center.

The couple pioneered the psychedelic movement and a part of the counterculture. They both experimented with synthetic mescaline shortly after the war and published their findings in a scientific paper that led to correspondence with such luminaries as Albert Einstein. "Magic" drinks, including mescaline mixtures, had long been used in Native American societies as a means of spiritual transformation, expanding consciousness and opening the soul's doors. Nan took mescaline "to enhance the images from my childhood memories and mysterious talks with the rainforest." She also tried LSD, which, she said, didn't agree with her. Above all, Nan's deep and central connection with the earth, nature, and living beings, learned as a child in the rainforests of Guatemala, would inform much of her worldview, and she expressed sadness at how people abused the sacred Mother Earth.

Georg was a self-taught Buddhist and believed his art could serve as a visual guide to the deeper, intuitive self and would inspire "truth seekers." According to his wife, he was "charismatic" and believed that his art and philosophy of life would guide others on a new path. Their book, ***In the Kingdom of Mescal***, became known as the hippie bible. Georg began to attract a group of people with similar views on life and formed a "clan," which drove a wedge between the couple and eventually led to their divorce. She lived in

Panajachel on Lake Atitlan until she died in 2019 at ninety-two.

In the Kingdom of Mescal, a psychedelic myth and an exotic work of art rooted in Nan's vision and her Maya culture can be found. One edition of the book includes a foreword by Guatemalan writer and Nobel Prize winner Miguel Angel Asturias, who met Nan and Georg in Paris when Asturias was the Guatemalan ambassador to France.

Many more twists and turns remain to be explored. How did the Maya/German cultural mix impact this tale? What other versions of the book are available? These are just a few mysteries surrounding this fascinating *Indian Fairy Tale for Adults*. But there can be no doubt that Nan and Georg's unique perspective and their experimentation with hallucinogenic drugs bore rare fruit, and art and literature were richer for it.

Chapter 2

MAYA GODS & MONSTERS: SUPERNATURAL STORIES FROM THE UNDERWORLD AND BEYOND

Lidar image technology and National Geographic specials have introduced many people to the ancient Maya civilization. This book invites even more readers into the worldview and the mystical realm that reflects the heart of the Maya people. Through captivating stories and exotic illustrations, it also draws upon ancient myths and lore and gives life to their quirky gods.

Michael Coe, respected anthropologist and author, says of *Maya Gods & Monsters*, "Inspired by myths, stories, and images from over two thousand years of Maya civilization and religious beliefs, Carol Karasik has given a highly readable and lively vision of the supernatural world of these remarkable people."

Karasik explains why the Maya have so many ceremonies to communicate with the underworld. "These stories have many versions. All these gods have many faces. Maya gods and goddesses live in a private world. They seldom interfere in the great and small affairs of humanity. They created human beings who would praise them—this is all. When not summoned through offerings and prayers, they keep to themselves...."

"Water Lily Jaguar swims in the silver pool of the moon...." is just one of fifteen stories that blend the natural and the supernatural within the world of the Maya.

The book also includes a brief history of the Maya, a map of Mesoamerica, a glossary, and a revealing piece titled "The Story of the Book," which explains the importance of the *Popol Vuh*, often called the Maya Bible. The author explains, "Mainly because the Hero Twins' selflessness and sacrifice offer moral lessons by which to live. The defeat of death is the theme of all religions. Readers don't have to believe in many creations to understand the cycle of life, death, and rebirth at the heart of the Maya philosophy..."

The dreamy figures depicted by Alfonso Huerta help spur one's imagination while being true to the colorful characters from the mythical Mesoamerican tradition. Huerta is a native of Mazatlán, Sinaloa, Mexico, and provides a unique artistic perspective, blending awareness of the beauty of everyday objects with surrealism and lush tropical colors.

Author Carol Karasik weaves together wise retellings of ancient stories based on the latest explorations of hieroglyphic texts and iconography, along with a profound understanding of the Maya's oral and written literary tradition.

She has published various books on Maya culture, such as the award-winning *Maya Threads: A Woven History of Chiapas*. The author is a poet, writer, and editor who has worked on books and films in anthropology, art, ecology, and educational philosophy.

Chapter 3

TIME AMONG THE MAYA: TRAVELS IN BELIZE, GUATEMALA, AND MEXICO PERSONAL REFLECTIONS

*The cover of the book which
ELAND Press published*

I came across this travel classic after writing an essay about author Moritz Thomsen, which was published in ELAND Press, and as a token of appreciation, the editor offered me any three of their books. This book, with the cover of the iconic Santo Tomás church in Chichicastenango, Quiché, filled with a mix of indigenous flowers and women in *traje* (traditional garb), and the smoke of incense emanating from the church, where chickens are often sacrificed on the top steps was my first choice. Very appropriate for a travel book that simultaneously covers the Old and New World, including the lives and culture of today's Maya.

Although I was managing programs in Sierra Leone, West Africa, when Ronald Wright wrote his book, I'd traveled to many places he describes, including the unforgettable Santo Tomás Hotel, where the author and team stayed. As the author explains, "There's hot water, colonial-style furniture, even a corner fireplace and a stack of logs. The room is arranged around patios full of flowers, stone fountains, and parrots on perches."

But he adds a critical caveat, which he addresses throughout the book: "It should be a delightful place, but now it feels tainted. According to human rights organizations, there were fifty-four massacres in Quiché during 1982 alone; more than three thousand civilians were killed." Also, throughout the book, Wright provides the sources for this disturbing reality—in this case, a report published by the Guatemalan Church in Exile. The author traveled through some of the communities hardest hit by violence, such as Nebaj and Uspantán, in the Department of Quiché, where I had worked in and around for many years.

He begins each chapter with Maya glyphs/script and explains their meaning. He also provides maps, a glossary, bibliography, and further readings—a comprehensive presentation.

Although I've studied the Maya and Guatemala in depth over the years and have a degree in Latin American Studies, I've rarely found such a mix of literary and historical materials as I did in Wright's book. Here's his description of the area outside of Chichicastenango, which still rang true when I visited several years ago:

Our room looks out on the canyons and the magnificent pine-bristled hills that climb out of them and stride toward the horizon. The cloud has lifted from the western mountains, allowing the sun to throw a weak coppery light on dark trees. Bright green clearings glow on the hillside wherever a farmer has a patch of young corn.

And of a Mayan shaman (priest) worshiping at a family shrine, "I notice other plumes of smoke, blue against the dirty clouds, rising from small fields higher up in the mountains. Apart from the worshipers, everything is still; one has the feeling of being in an enchanted place, a land of ancient numina."

The author takes the reader to Tikal: "Here on their tallest building, in their greatest metropolis, I'm at the center of the Maya world," and describes the panoramic setting as follows:

From the top, the forest stretches to the horizon on all sides, diaphanous waves of mist washing across it like an ocean swell. The dark canopy, showing through in lacy troughs, hints at bottomless green depths, and from these rises the steep islands of the five great pyramids.

The author transports us to the ruins of Iximché, outside Tejutlá on the Pan-American highway: "Iximché is a tranquil park, about a mile long and up to a quarter-mile wide. Remains of temples, palace platforms, and two ball-courts stand whitely among well-mowed lawns. Stands of *ocote* and Caribbean pine cover what were once suburbs and the cliffs protecting the Cakchiquel stronghold. A raven's croak echoes in the woods..."

The journey through Guatemala takes on a different tone as the author learns of the devastating period of violence, which he witnessed first-hand as he traveled through in the early 1980s. The afterward section of the 2020 edition of the book published by Eland Press refers to the United

Nations Truth Commission in 1999, which summed up the impact as: "93% of civilian killings between 1961 and 1996 - more than 200,000 all said - were the work of Guatemala state forces, often with the United States and other foreign support. More than four-fifths of the victims were Maya."

Wright provides the backdrop for the circumstances that led to this level of killing by the Kaibiles, or "Tigers," crack counterinsurgency troops modeled on the Green Berets, with this responsorial chant at a training camp:

What does a Kaibil eat?
FLESH.
What kind of flesh?
HUMAN!
What kind of flesh?
COMMUNIST...

The author quotes a report that a survivor of the July 1982 massacre at the village of San Francisco in the Department of Huehuetenango said he saw a soldier cut out the heart of a warm corpse and put it into his mouth. The real tragedy is that the term "Kaibiles" (Mayan, Mam leader) has been appropriated to describe a group composed basically of Ladinos (non-Maya Guatemalans, as well as Mayas who have adopted non-Maya cultural/social norms). "The atrocities allegedly committed by them and other army units are like the early accounts of Nazi horrors, strain the belief of anyone living far from the social climate in which they took place. But reports are many and detailed."

One of the author's stories brought back memories of my visits to the coffee plantation on the southern slopes of the Volcano of Atitlán, San Francisco Miramar, owned by my wife's grandfather. During the civil war, the guerrilla group ORPA (Organization of People in Arms) partially occupied the area, so they'd come in during the day to talk with the workers, followed in the afternoon by members of the Guatemalan army. During this period, an honorary consul of Norway lost his life when his small plane landed at the neighboring Finca Panamá for a visit. He was attacked by members of ORPA, who thought the plane was part of a military operation. It was a tumultuous time, and the Norwegian consul was in the wrong place at the wrong time, which could happen to anyone.

I always appreciate the insights a British-born traveler like Wright brings when describing the role of the U.S. in violence because of their unique, usually better-informed perspective. The United Fruit Company and the U.S. government justified much of the killing due to a "communist threat," which the author sums up as, "The political current flows south, not north. The idea that Nicaragua, El Salvador, or Guatemala might spread some ideological contagion northward through Mexico to the gringo empire is the most ludicrous paranoia. Unfortunately for Central America, the United States suffers from what Carlos Fuentes has called "unabashed historical amnesia."

What impresses me the most about Wright's book is the author's ability to pinpoint some of the critical issues that impacted the countries he visited in the 1980s and continue, in many ways, to influence the situation in Central America today. Like most countries in Latin America, he points out that Guatemala had a "paper" country and a "real" one. The paper Guatemala, with its constitution, a system of justice, and primarily free elections, existed alongside the real Guatemala where "selfish interests seize power and hold it by corruption and terror. The two countries pulled in opposite directions—one belonged to the military regime, the other to the insurgents; one was urban, the other rural; one depended on infrastructure—roads, airstrips, open fields; the other thrived in the wilderness. This is not a new pattern: it has been the fundamental structure of the Guatemalan conquest-state since 1524."

The author calls "Ladinoization" a process of overt racism and persecution. The Ladinos use European attire and speak Spanish, and determining the percentage of the population, which is still Maya, is complicated because, under certain circumstances, they become Ladinos. "In Guatemala, as in other Latin American countries, 'race' is more a matter of culture than genetics: one is an Indian because one defines oneself by wearing the clothes, speaking the language, and keeping to the values and traditions that symbolize Indian ethnicity."

Historically, the role of epidemics in bringing down much of the Indigenous community in Guatemala was breathtaking, "...between 1520 and 1600, their populations fell by about ninety percent. At least forty or fifty million people must have died...." It was the most significant demographic collapse in human history: proportionally three times more severe than the Black Death, severely disrupting medieval Europe without an accompanying invasion. "Great was the stench of the dead," recalled the Annals of the Cakchiquels. The plague referred to was probably smallpox.

Another insight Wright offers into the life of the Maya is that their greatest strength and weakness was their disunity. "They could not be subdued like the Aztecs by the destruction of a single city, nor paralyzed like the Incas by the ransom of a god-king. But their internecine squabbles closed their eyes to the Spanish threat until it was too late."

This diversity is reflected in the twenty-four different languages the Maya speak. The author illustrates this with a language chart of essential, traditional words in each language. The terms of the Ixil and Quiché (roughly from the same area) are very different from the language of the Maya in the Yucatan.

This contrasts with the legacy of the Inca Empire of Quechua and the Bolivians' state bilingualism. "So, the Maya has been condemned by history to the margins of the modern world. But, like the Welsh, the Maya do not give up their culture easily."

The complex world of religion among the Maya is adeptly illustrated through the Catholic Church's image in Santiago on the shores of Lake Atitlán. The church was built in 1568 and "is full of ancient and bizarre wooden saints propped against the walls. They are not static or serene, but stooping, writhing, dancing, oozing a glutinous blend of sanity and pain." These "saints" are cared for by a Maya organization called a *cofradia*, a Catholic brotherhood organized to carry out charitable acts, which has been the basis of local government.

This practice was a form of ancestor worship to the Catholic hierarchy, and the most crucial ancestor was "Maximón." Catholics told the author that Maximón was an "effigy of Judas Iscariot." But experts say his name is a conflation of San Simón and Max, a Mayan word for tobacco. The Maximón I have visited in Santiago appears with a big cigar between his wooden lips - like the ancient Death Lords - and his followers bestow him with many meanings and roles.

Wright recognizes the complexity and danger he encountered on his trip with his comment when departing: "At midnight, I walk across the international bridge. A small boy changes the last of my quetzals for pesos. Mexico! Suddenly I realize I've been holding my breath for weeks."

In the epilogue, Wright states, "The modern Maya are traveling many roads: the hard road of armed resistance, the quiet road of refuge, the seductive road of accommodation.... On my journey, I have not found what I feared: that the Maya face extinction - much more than the rest of us. If there is to be the twenty-first century, the Maya will be part of it...."

Through all the complexity Wright encountered during his trek through Mexico, Guatemala, and Belize, he identified with the problem expressed by Gabriel García Márquez, who said that Latin American writers' significant issue is not to create fantasy from what is real, "but to make Latin America's reality believable - a much more difficult task," which Ronald Wright did admirably. And I agree with Jan Morris of The Independent London, who says, "*Time Among the Maya* shows Wright to be far more than a mere storyteller or descriptive writer. He is a historical philosopher with a profound understanding of other cultures."

Ronald Wright is the author of ten books of fiction, history, essays, and travel published in eighteen languages and over forty countries. His first novel, *A Scientific Romance*, won Britain's David Higham Prize for Fiction and was chosen as a Book of the Year by *The Sunday Times* and the *New York Times*. Wright's CBC Massey Lectures, *A Short History of Progress*, won the Libris Award for Nonfiction Book of the Year and inspired Martin Scorsese's 2011 documentary, *Surviving Progress*. His other bestsellers include *Time Among the Maya* and *Stolen Continents*, chosen as a Book of the Year by *The Independent* and *The Sunday Times*. His latest work is *The Gold Eaters*, a novel set during the Spanish invasion of the Inca Empire. Born in England to British and Canadian parents, Wright lives on Canada's west coast.

Chapter 4

VICTOR MONTEJO'S DREAM FOR A SECURE MAYA COMMUNITY

*Victor Montejo with the sculp-
ture of Don Quixote*

I first became aware of Victor Montejo almost twenty years ago when I read *The Adventures of Mr. Puttison Among the Maya*, his historical and satirical novel about an American traveler who turns up in a remote Maya village and is mistakenly thought to be a priest, sewing confusion among the local population.

The story provides an excellent example of how the Maya and Western worldviews can collide. The book is beautifully written, comical in places, yet reveals much about the Maya people and the injustices they have endured over the centuries.

One of my favorite scenes reflects the cultural differences between the Maya and "outsiders," which is the basis of many Maya communities' mistrust with the outside world. Dudley, the outsider/traveler, takes a skull from a local ceremonial cave, which he doesn't think is a big deal. Soon after, he is bitten by a snake and is treated by a local Maya "healer." Hallucinating, Dudley describes a strange dream: A woman in traditional Maya clothing beseeches him to return the skull he has taken. Dudley had not thought taking the head was a problem. The locals feel otherwise: "Well, maybe it's not a problem for you, but it is for us because we respect the memory of our ancestors, and we know that they watch over and protect us from wherever they are, and we respect them and remember them every moment of our existence."

At the end of the book, Puttison's "adventures" take a very dark turn as Dudley invites two friends to stay with him. Together they pillage the local cave where many artifacts and religious items are kept: "The three foreigners then dragged the sack into the bushes and ... divided up its contents. Each one carried his share, and...they headed up a shortcut through the mountains to the Mexican border. Like souls possessed by the devil, the three thieves began to run like crazy, trying to get out of Guatemala as quickly as possible."

I revisited the book in English while researching a documentary I have been collaborating on about the impact of migration on Maya communities, "Guatemala: Trouble in the Highlands." Our production team was interested in Professor Montejo because we felt Maya intellectuals like him would best be able to tell the story of the challenges that impact the Maya community, particularly endemic racism and political and economic inequalities, historical realities that have not changed much in over four hundred years.

Through the ensuing research, Victor Montejo's compelling personal life story also began to unfold. Born in 1951 in a poor Maya village in the Guatemalan highlands, he was a schoolteacher during the bloody Guatemalan Civil War. In 1982, he and his family had to flee to Mexico. Over a decade of enormous struggles, they were helped by a series of American benefactors. He learned English and, with intellectual drive, persistence, and good luck, earned a Ph.D. in anthropology. In addition to teaching for many years at prestigious American universities and writing many academic treatises, he became a scholar, poet, children's story writer, and significant Maya public intellectual, recognized nationally and internationally. His writings provide invaluable insights into the Maya world.

Montejo returned to Guatemala in 2004 to influence the direction of the post-Civil War government in its efforts to establish a peace accord. He won the Guatemalan National Congress seat and was named Minister of Peace from this post. He worked on the National Program for Reparation to the victims of the armed conflict in Guatemala and was named President of the Congressional Commission of Indigenous People.

As a congressman, he proposed and passed the National Day of Indigenous People of Guatemala law and proposed the law initiative: The Law to Consult Indigenous Communities. The second Montejo book I read, *Testimony: Death of a Guatemalan Village,* is accurately critiqued by Third World Resources, which states, "One would be hard-pressed to cram more suspense and drama between the covers of a 120-page book than Victor Montejo has done in *Testimony.*"

The author's "Dedication" to this book reflects his motivation for writing it:

I dedicate this book
To the memory

> *Of the many thousand*
> *Guatemalans*
> *Who were killed or disappeared*
> *During this decade*
> *Of aggression and struggle.*
> *And even*
> *If there are attempts*
> *To blot out their names.*
> *Little by little*
> *I know that wildflowers*
> *Are growing daily*
> *From their clandestine bones-*
> *They were scattered there in the ravines and the moun-*
> *tains.*

Montejo, a local schoolteacher at the time, takes us to a remote village in the northwest department of Huehuetenango. No movie houses, theaters, television, electric lights, drinking water, or highways exist. According to Montejo:

> *The only access to this community is a narrow, twist-*
> *ing road that crosses streams and deep gullies as they*
> *climb high into the craggy uplands. Few of the villagers*
> *complete the sixth grade in school, as most abandon*
> *classes after third and fourth grades, not because they do*
> *not like schoolwork but because they must accompany*
> *their parents on their migration to the distant coast*
> *plantations.*

One of the real tragedies of the Guatemalan Civil War, which lasted from 1960 to 1996, was the Guatemalan military's strategy of choosing poorly trained local men to be the "civil patrols," with a vague mandate to "protect" their communities against communist insurgents. On September 9, 1982, the civil patrol of Montejo's village of Tzalala mistook an army detachment dressed in olive fatigues for guerrillas, and all hell broke loose. Soon after, army officers arrived in the village with a "blacklist" of suspects, members of the local civil patrol—in other words, neighbors "ratted" on neighbors.

Victor Montejo was brought to an army base, where he heard an interrogation in the process:

> *The wails of the unfortunate man got lost in the night's sepulchral silence. The barking of dogs in nearby houses was the only response to the bone-chilling howls, which died down gradually, like a radio whose volume is progressively lowered until soundless. I shuddered to think of the fate of that luckless man after they finished with him. First, they cut out one eye, then the other. Then the nose, lips, tongue, ears and testicles, and at last they sliced off his head. It is a slow, excruciating death, conceived to make a human being die in the greatest possible pain.*

Montejo was released unharmed, but the local situation deteriorated quickly. The author realized he had to go somewhere else to protect his life, "and so one night I fled with my wife and children in the firm expectation of returning when peace and tranquility will have returned to the beloved land of the quetzal."

Inspired by his experience living in a U.N.-sponsored refugee camp in Chiapas, Mexico, Montejo wrote his next book, *Voices from Exile: Violence and Survival in Modern Maya History*, to give voice to those Maya villagers. They were forced to remain silent for so long because of fears of reprisal and violence. He combines autobiographical history, political analysis, and a powerful testimonial narrative to explore this state of terror and its inescapable human cost.

Although this book was written over twenty years ago, it is both timely and compelling, given that the author is from Jacaltenango, Huehuetenango, in the Guatemalan Highlands, and was a first-hand eyewitness to the violence, which, to a degree, still occurs today. "Voices from Exile" won the National Race, Ethnicity, and Politics Award from the American Political Science Association.

Montejo provides the historical backdrop to the refugees fleeing their country, including the long-standing tradition of forced labor of the Maya population and the long series of indigenous uprisings. As the author points out, even independence did not change the conditions of the Indigenous Maya communities.

Initially, Maya refugees living in Mexican camps for displaced persons could not return to their country because of the ongoing violence and prejudices that awaited them. When they could return, they found their lands had been stolen. Finally, in the mid-1980s, Costa Rica President Oscar Arias led a series of discussions, resulting in the Central American Peace Accord, signed in August of 1987 by all six Central American country's presidents. After that, almost 2,500 returnees, including Victor and his family, were accompanied home by 240 international observers.

A respected anthropologist from Brown University, Kay Warren, sums up the next Montejo book I reviewed, *Maya Intellectual Renaissance: Identity Representation and Leadership*, as follows: "This striking project will be of broad interest to scholars and students concerned with social movements and indigenous rights. The topic is important and timely, and the author is one of the most respected Maya intellectuals and activists."

I especially appreciated the author's insights because I have worked throughout the highlands of Guatemala, starting with the Peace Corps in the early '70s. However, I never stayed in one place long enough to learn any of the twenty-two languages and cultural complexities of the various Maya linguistic groups in the country. Montejo's understanding of the Maya worldview is impressive. He brings a clear vision of a new political alternative for the future of a movement that promotes inter-ethnic collaboration alongside a reverence for Maya culture.

This book is the first to be published outside of Guatemala, in which a Maya writer other than Rigoberta Menchú (a Nobel Peace Prize winner) discusses the history and problems of the country. It contains essays Montejo has written over the past ten years that address three critical issues facing Maya people today: identity, representation, and Maya leadership. He explores the realities of the ancient and contemporary Maya worlds. He is deeply involved in furthering the discussion of the effectiveness of Maya's leadership because he believes that self-evaluation is necessary for the movement to advance.

One part of the book explores the role of non-Maya scholars in the Maya and how some of the actual icons, such as the influential scholar, Sylvanus G. Morley, whose writings on cultural image and history were based on the Yukatek Maya area, became the prototype for all Mayan, "extending beyond Yucatan and encompassing all thirty-one modern Maya linguistic communities in the region." Like many Maya scholars, Morley relied heavily on material provided by Diego de Landa, the colonial Spanish Bishop of Yucatan, whose campaigns against idolatry resulted in the burning of almost all the Mayan codices (manuscripts).

According to Montejo, by establishing historical facts in ethnographies, scholars have helped to distort the image of the ancient Maya and that of the present Maya. Montejo believes that racism in Guatemala is best understood as a system originating from the Spanish conquest inequality. The Spanish view of Indigenous people was that of barbarians who needed to be controlled and civilized; to accomplish this, they created the *encomienda*, forced labor based on a European feudal system.

Montejo goes on to say:

> *The interplay of class and ethnicity in Guatemala is somewhat ambivalent. There are class differences among the elite and the ladino (Europeanized local population), and the oligarchy is composed primarily of twenty-two families of European background. And most importantly, Indigenous people have been rejected as active participants in the country's social, economic, and political life. A hegemonic nationalism has been*

created in which the ancient Maya are glorified, and the present Maya are disdained and discriminated against.

Among the leaders promoting and defining the Maya people are the ajq'ij, or Maya priests, who have become a symbol of rebirth and unification of the Maya culture on a national level. Montejo is a great proponent of "Pan Mayanism" as well, a vision of the future of the Maya people. The author lists vital tenets, such as "reaffirming that we are Maya like our ancestors, recognizing that Maya culture is not a monopoly of a single Maya group, and making the diversity of Maya cultures visible." According to the author, this shared culture should be recognized by "maintaining equality and respect for differences and cultural particularities." This pan-Maya culture will lay the foundation for the construction of a Guatemalan nationalism that is multicultural, where Maya and non-Maya are treated equally.

Above all, the author sees himself as the protector of the Maya culture. In *Sculpted Stones*, a collection of twenty-six of his poems, Montejo, a Jakaltek Maya, vividly expresses the values of traditional Maya culture while simultaneously exposing the brutal thirty-six-year war of extermination people endured.

Here is an amazing poem from *Sculpted Stones*:

Lost in the jungle—several millennia
of history,and forgotten by men—
shining millenniaof victory.
The Maya and their glyphs
stand as one
like fathers and sons
measuring the present
in the easy-going eyes
of the tourist
who stands by a stele
in Tikal stroking
a round glyph
which bares its teeth
to the onlookers

as if saying:
After two thousand years,
traveler,
we're still on our feet
vigilant
among the silken
cobwebs
of time...

Finally, I came across an essay by Montejo in *The Rigob-erta Menchú Controversy*, edited by Arturo Arias. This dialectic collection followed Indigenous rights activist Rigoberta Menchú's memoir, which focused world attention on Guatemala and led to her being awarded the Nobel Peace Prize in 1992. In 1999, a North American anthropologist, David Stoll, challenged the veracity of key details in Menchú's account. Journalists and scholars squared off regarding whether Menchú had lied about her past and, if so, what that would mean about the larger truths revealed in her book. The controversy led to harsh critiques from both the political right and left. Victor Montejo's response reflected a different take on the "sacrilege" of questioning Menchú's stories. Montejo says, "They have forgotten that all writings are "suspicious" and that they represent the political or ideological conditioning or tendencies of the individual who produces them."

He goes on to say,

"It seems that those who promoted the guerrilla war internationally are now without much to do, and this is the opportunity to keep fighting and firing from their computers the Maya movement. They are not interested in the Maya's problems now in Guatemala. For the Maya, the ex-guerrillas and the government are seen as political tricksters who have been deceiving the people.

"The Maya want to be in charge of their projects and now are struggling to make the Guatemalan govern-

ment comply with the peace accords and the reparation recommendations of the CEH. The Menchú-Stoll controversy is only entertainment for academics and politicians who want to accuse each other or themselves of what they have failed to do, namely, to work with Indigenous people.

"Engaging in this kind of debate distends ourselves from the reality that Indigenous people live in. We know that they suffered the most and were targeted for destruction because of their ethnicity. And we are aware that no one is being prosecuted for these criminal actions..."

Although Montejo left a successful university teaching job in the U.S. to return to his Maya community in Jacaltenango, his three children did not. All three have established successful careers in the U.S. One is a doctor, another is a medical administrator, and the third is a teacher and artist. I recently asked Montejo how he explained their success, despite the traumatic circumstances of their initial exile from Guatemala.

Here is Montejo's explanation of this success:

I am blessed to have three children who went through school in the United States, from primary education to university, without problems. I think they also followed my example in pursuing higher education. Despite being an adult, and considering the cultural and language barrier, I managed to learn the language and pursue a Ph.D. in anthropology. Why anthropology? Because to me it was the most immediate way to get success in the United States. I realized that most anthropologists do not know the culture and the language and are successful with their career. Why not me if I am a Maya descendant? I know and live my culture, the Mayan language. It seemed the obvious way to go in search of a professional career to survive in the United States.

For me, the U.S. is a beautiful country, and it has many opportunities; I wanted to share my Maya culture from the inside, teaching and producing literary and academic works that are pursued at different universities. That's why my children followed their desire to get the best education they could, since they speak English, Spanish, and a Mayan language. They had to struggle for themselves to achieve their goals and even got student loans to achieve their university educations, as any U.S. student with limited resources. We never used public welfare because we preferred to work hard instead.

In the case of my oldest boy, he wanted to be a doctor since he was a child. He was hospitalized at the Maryknoll hospital. A Maryknoll sister/doctor, Sister Rose, attended him all the time and when she asked what he wanted to be, he said, "I want to become a doctor like you." She was happy to learn this before she died.

My daughter always liked to draw. Eventually, she became an artist and a schoolteacher in California. She also painted the scene that became the cover of my **Adventures of Mr. Puttison** *book.*

To this day, Montejo considers that the task before him is the elimination of racism and discrimination, a first step toward creating a Guatemala with respectful relationships between Mayas and Ladinos and the elimination of economic barriers for the Maya.

With economic self-sufficiency and appropriate higher education, Indigenous people can shatter the ethnic tension and prejudice against them. Education is one primary tool to move toward genuine ethnic reaffirmation and obtain access to economic and political power in our country but achieving this is difficult. At the same time, the Maya majority remains mired in poverty in the most remote rural areas of the country. Past governments have not worried about Indigenous people

> *and have kept them powerless as second-class citizens. And when Mayas criticize their oppressors, they are often accused of being racists or of promoting reverse racism. Another important tool for us is auto criticism and ethnocentrism. Self-criticism and introspection are necessary to understand ourselves and others as we recognize our failures and achievements, not only as Maya but as Guatemalans.*

Victor Montejo continues to be a prolific writer. His most recently published book, ***Secuestro a Ultratumba***, was published by Windmills International. Another book, ***Ixim: La Leyenda del Descubrimiento del Maiz***, is currently in a Guatemalan publishing house. A newly completed academic title, ***Mayalogue: An Interactionist Theory of Indigenous Cultures***, is being considered for publication by SUNY-Press. In the future, he wants to combine his poems into one book. He is also working on a memoir, **With One Foot in Two Worlds.**

Chapter 5

ALLEGRO TO GUATEMALA: AN EXPATRIATE JOURNEY THROUGH THE LAND OF ETERNAL SPRING

Earl and Suzanne de Berge in Antigua, Guatemala

Most of the more than 6,000 U.S. expatriates who live in Guatemala have a distinct way of appreciating and expressing their love for Guatemala. Several years ago, I met poet

Earl Vincent de Berge and his wife, Suzanne, over lunch in Phoenix to discuss fundraising strategies for Seeds for a Future, a non-governmental organization (NGO) they set up in Guatemala. I soon learned that we shared a love and appreciation for Guatemala and the Desert Southwest, and that Earl was also a writer, in his case, poetry.

So, I was surprised to learn that he started writing back in 1959. This summer, he is publishing ***A Finger of Land on an Old Man's Hand***, an autographical novel laced with poetry and photos about his adventures as a young man in the Sonoran deserts of Baja, California, Mexico, and Arizona. As a high school senior, Earl came across one of the great Chinese poets, Li Po, noted for his elegant romantic verse, which he felt compelled to express to some of the various women in his life. Earl wrote about nature, the environment, cities, and social issues. His travels through Central America, the Sonoran Desert, and the Andes fueled his imagination. "Everything I experience has potential for a poem—even the increasingly dreadful business of politics."

In ***Allegro to Life***, Earl's poems are divided into "Songs from my Life," "Poems from Guatemala," and "Desert Songs." From the Desert Southwest, the author transports us to the unique, ever-moist environs of the rainforest in Guatemala with "Chipi-Chipi:"

CHIPI-CHIPI
It is raining/ in the way of mist,/ just heavy enough/ to cling to plants/ ...too light to dimple the lake...

Chipi-Chipi is the name/ Tzutujil speakers/ give to mist rain/ that neither/ starts nor stops/ yet accumulates/ like dew/ to drip gently from/ palm fronds./ One senses eternity.

For years, the author and his wife split their time between Guatemala and Arizona and have owned a home on Lake Atitlán, but eventually were drawn to Antigua, so I wasn't surprised to find this enchanting tale of life in the Central Plaza there:

BLIND IN ANTIGUA
Girdled by ancient Spanish buildings, / their silent arches like eyes gazing with/ stern conqueror authority into Antigua's / grace-

ful central park where modern folks/ now stroll, dally, and relax beneath gnarled jacaranda trees in full lavender flower...

In slow waltz, the calm mix of humanity stirs/ in social mingling, a seamless stream that eddies, / and pauses on benches where lovers giggle/ and women chat in clusters, their hands waving/ "oh really!" as they rock back laughing in/ the glow of fresh neighborhood chin-wagging...

A man sits with sad, slumped shoulders/ one foot raised on the shoeshine boy's box/ as he reads of war and butchery in the world./ Worried only about future family meals.

A poem Earl wrote on the arm-in-arm Sunday sauntering of "muchacha's" brought back fond memories of my participation in this historic tradition.

THE CENTRAL PARK RAINBOW

Antigua's central plaza is a rainbow of so many curious people that I am guilty of surreptitiously studying, many as unobtrusively as an older gent can.

The rainbow faces are electric:
... friendly, with gender politics low-keyed.
... bored, seeking a conversation.
... amused and sexily attired.
... insistent aloofness.
... contemptuous when noticed.
... strutters on the hunt.
... tourists behind cameras.
... peanut peddlers.
... jewelry and scarf sellers.
... evangelicals preaching damnation.
... children selling gum and cigarettes.
... jugglers and guitarists.
... children with animated minion dolls.
... toddlers with soap-bubble squirt guns.
... small-bag coffee merchants.
... shy Maya families from the countryside.
... cops running off drunks.
... 20s glued to ear-buds.
... old gringos jawing tall tales.
... oblivious lovers.
... and slack faced daydreamers.
... they all seem so relaxed.

Few will forget the Easter pageantry of "Semana Santa" (Holy Week) in Antigua, expressed so well in the following poem:

GOOD FRIDAY ANTIGUA

I imagine myself hefting the huge anda —
leaning into the swirl of blue incense,
my hand, white gloved at my cheek
lifting in lock step with eighty men
the weight of Jesus bearing the cross,
my mind on this day of His passion
— my day of repentance and devotion.

Approaching the central cathedral,
walking over alfombras of flowered devotion,
cucuruchos guard our path against
gawking tourists, clicking cameras,
patronizing grins, uncovered heads
and I love New York T-shirts.

Incense cleanses the air,
blurs my view of tourist faces
leaning into the veil of incense
as if watching us gives them
understanding of faith.

The crowd fades to silhouettes
— then into nothing
as the rhythm and sway of we eighty
pulls me back into Jesus and his love.

Earl then deftly takes us from the enchanting world of Antigua to Guatemala's troubled, violent past during the civil war in the 1980s.

CESSPOOL BRAIN

Imagine,/ if you can, the cesspool brain/ of the Guatemalan army colonel/ who ordered the murder/ of hundreds of Indigenous/ civilians and their burial/ in his army's latrine pits.
Imagine again/ if you can,/ him walking away./ Whistling of a job well done./ Time will fade victims' names/ and the pain of personal loss/ but the Maya have not forgotten the/ meaning of their agony./ Genocide is the mother of the next war.

Earl uses the plain language, "My Texas mother can understand." He uses metaphors and rhyming sparingly. No matter where the poem occurs, it is underscored with a clear idea, image, and emotion, which paint a picture that will send the reader adrift on their journey.

One astute reader says: His economy of words—reminiscent of Asian and Native American poetry—thrusts the reader directly into the subject, whether it be the blessing of rain on a thirsty desert cactus or the grief of a soul destroyed by Guatemala's Civil War. Earl's uncluttered directness embodies what Thomas Merton, author of the spiritual classic, *The Seven Story Mountain,* said of his artist father: "His vision was religious and clean, and therefore his paintings were without decoration or superfluous comment since a religious man respects the power of God's creation to bear witness for itself."

Suzanne de Berge is the driving force and president of Seeds for a Future. A graduate of Antioch College, Suzanne combined her liberal arts education with interests in science, native cultures, and the natural world.

In 2004, Suzanne and Earl volunteered at a Pre-Classic Maya archaeology site beneath the village of Chocolá on the south coast of Guatemala. Working side-by-side with people from the modern-day town kindled their interest in helping their new friends have healthier and more prosperous lives.

Joined by other archaeology volunteers in 2007, they formed Seeds for a Future, a U.S. non-profit. Seeds provides affordable and sustainable training to impoverished rural women in and around Chocolá to improve family access to food and nutrition. Suzanne said "We knew that we wanted a self-help program for families. They could build their futures and create success using the skills and confidence gained through knowledge and experience." As Seeds approaches the fifteen-year mark, it is supported by contributions from individuals across the U.S. and beyond, and is drawing attention from health and nutrition organizations in Central America. I found the food security component of the work timely, since 47% of Guatemalan children are malnourished, with malnutrition increasing since 2015, according to the UN's World Food Program. If that's not bad enough, "stunting" among Guatemalan children is at one of the highest rates in the world.

I also appreciated that the program is staffed by local Guatemalans who are a part of the community. Their training and experience as extensionist agents make them a vital community resource, coaching and mentoring families to become self-reliant and prosperous. Each year, a core of twelve to twenty families complete a twelve-month training and mentoring program in each village. Many of these families share their new skills with family, friends, and neighbors, creating real and lasting change through knowledge and self-reliance in communities where many children face chronic malnutrition and where families once had limited options. The de Berges are proud of the Seeds for a Future field team and their success in helping families build better lives.

For example, Clelia Ixquiatap, the project coordinator and a senior extensionist, received extensive nutrition training as part of the INCAP (Nutrition Institute for Central America and Panama)/Nestle project, which evaluated the Seeds for a Future program's impact on local nutrition and health. Clelia was vital to transferring nutrition information to the study's participants and continues in that role with today's participating families.

The ethnic diversity of the communities they served also fascinated the de Berges, as it did me. Most of the area's population is Maya Kaqchikel. However, in the 1880s, German owners of Finca Chocolá, a cattle and coffee plantation, brought in workers from Quiché, resulting in an "island" of K'iche' speakers in a sea of Kaqchikel. So, in a few thousand years, you go from ancient Maya/Olmec to Maya Kaqchikel, and thanks to the Germans, to Maya Q'iche - all in the same community.

Enchanted by the gentle people, their culture, and a spectacular natural environment, Earl and Suzanne created a program that helps rural Guatemalan families build better lives for themselves and their children. Earl's poetry allowed him to express his insights on Guatemala in a most lyrical manner, while Suzanne saw herself through her community-based programs.

As Earl and Suzanne reach their later years, they focus more on defining their legacy. This poem reflects how Earl puts their life's work into perspective:

ALL JOYOUS FRIENDS
All the joyous friends we know in life
Will fade, for who can outpace
the extinction mortals must face?
Death is a sequel to elude in pursuit
of selfless works in life that we cherish
until the knot of life unravels.
How can we help protect God's exposition that is life in nature?
How can we make ourselves one with God?
Selfless charity without command are
the joyous deeds not undone by death.
When we become one, our faults
are nothing against the virtue of true
charity in protecting nature.

Chapter 6

UNCOVERING THE ART OF FRANCISCO GOLDMAN

The recent HBO documentary, ***The Art of Political Murder***, introduced a growing number of readers to the author of the book on which it's based, Guatemalan American writer Francisco Goldman. Given his background - Guatemalan mother, Jewish-American father, and formative years growing up in rough and tumble Boston—Goldman has a unique insight into the violent history of Guatemala and what makes the country tick. The HBO documentary closely follows Goldman's book, a thorough dissection of the sensational murder of Guatemalan Bishop Juan Gerardi in 1998. Days before his brazen murder, Bishop Gerardi published a detailed account of the country's military involvement in the atrocities committed during Guatemala's civil war.

I was drawn to the author because, like Goldman's father, I married a Guatemalan woman. Like Goldman, my wife and our children bridge two cultures. And, like any culturally diverse family, there's always the sense of being somewhat of an outsider in both cultures.

Goldman's debut novel, **The Long Night of White Chickens,** published in 1992, foreshadowed some of the themes that piqued his interests as a journalist writing for top-tier magazines like *Harper's* and *The New Yorker,* and as a novelist.

In the novel, Goldman draws from his own experiences. The protagonist, Roger Graetz, is raised in a Boston suburb by a matriarchal Guatemalan mother. Into the household enters Flor de Mayo, a beautiful young Guatemalan orphan sent by his grandmother in Guatemala to serve as a maid. Years later, Flor is murdered in Guatemala, and Roger, devastated by the death of someone he secretly loved, travels to Guatemala to uncover how and why she was murdered. With the help of a childhood friend, he ventures on a quest to find Flor's murderer, a fascinating investigation in which myth intermingles with reality.

Goldman's attraction to this storyline reflects his interest in the Central American wars he covered in the 1980s as a *Harper's Magazine* journalist." As he says in a Lit Hub interview, "Sometimes people want to mystify where novels come from, but often novels come from the obvious source, simply what the writer is most persistently thinking about."

[]The *San Francisco Review of Books* said of the novel, "Not since Nabokov's infamous *Lolita* or Toni Morrison's *Song of Solomon* has an author displayed such mastery of contemporary literary methods."

Say Her Name (2011), Goldman's second novel, is an autobiographical, evocative story of love and loss. Goldman had married Mexican writer Aura Estrada, but tragically, a month before their second wedding anniversary, Aura died in a surfing accident. To exorcise the madness of grief and guilt, Goldman wrote a novel that creates a moving portrait of his love for Aura and utilizes humor and humility to lighten the pain he was experiencing due to her death. In the novel, he has a visceral reaction to a dream in which he has a conversation with Aura's spirit:

> *...I woke before dawn to find Aura stretched out beside me in our bed, nearly invisible, lighter darkness within the darkness of the room but with her distinct shape.... Did you just come in from the tree? I asked Aura. No, she said. Mi Amor, that's your imagination. Pobrecito, she giggled. Why would I want to hide in a tree in the middle of winter? So this is my imagination, too? No, this is me. Of course, it is. Aura, do you promise? Si, mi amor, it's me. I don't get it. If you can visit me like you are now, then why don't you come all the time? I've been so lonely without you. We're not allowed out that often, she said. If I were here all the time, then I would be a ghost, and I don't want to be a ghost. Ghosts suffer. That makes sense, I said. And, I thought, it really does make sense. But with that, Aura was gone, dispelled back into the air, into the chilled early morning light.*

The blend of Yankee investigative reporter and Latin mythmaker is an essential element of Goldman's most recent book, ***Monkey Boy*** (2021), which delves into his reflections on growing up in Boston, the quiet dark-skinned boy sitting in the back of the class, the "monkey boy." Like ***The Long Night of White Chickens***, it is designated as a novel, rather than an autobiography. In a revealing interview with Rachel Kushner for Lit Hub, Goldman explains the importance of changing the surname "Goldman" of his lead character:

> *So, yeah, that "-man" to "-berg" [Goldman to Goldberg] makes a big difference. It's a first decisive step into fiction, into turning myself into a character that's going to move and act and think within fiction. It's freeing myself from "myself," from any duty to be faithful to the "known facts," as I might be if I were writing an autobiography, even if many of the components I may be giving to "Frankie Goldberg" are, in fact, drawn from my own life.*

Walking the fine line between literary fiction and autobiography, bordering on realistic realism, allows the author to fill in gaps with fictional material that enhances the story. In an author interview published in *Identity Theory* magazine with Robert Birnbaum, Goldman claims that he agrees with Henry James that the historical novel is humbug. Henry James referred to the historical novel where people believed you could have a realist historical novel.

In the Lit Hub interview, Goldman explains the critical role that several women play in the story - Aura, his mother, his sister, and his grandmother:

> *There's also my Guatemalan grandmother, Abuelita, definitely a strong and eccentric woman who I adored, and the women she sent up to Boston to help my mother with housework and looking after us so that she could go to college, eventually becoming a college Spanish professor.*

In **Monkey Boy**, Frankie Goldberg visits two of these women:

> *As an adolescent, I had a talent for turning unrequited loves into friendships. Later my friendships with women didn't require such painful beginnings. All my adult life, I've also had strong male friendships in the U.S., Mexico, and Central America. But in the U.S.,*

most of my closest friends are women. I guess I enjoy their conversation, sense of humor, and way of being in the world more, and so relate to them more.

Jewish-Italian writer Natalia Ginzburg helped Goldman learn one crucial lesson related to his roots in a diverse, cultural background: *"How artificial the racial and ethnic categories we're boxed into are, and that there's no such thing as being 'half and half' anything, that we're only fully what and who we are."*

Goldman reveals interesting connections between his family and friends and critical events in Guatemala's history and shows how he can speculate about what might have been by fictionalizing his personal experiences and understanding based on his years covering Guatemala's corrupt elite class, army, and politicians:

Did the United Fruit bilingual secretary, Lolita Ojito, ever filch a note or diary page in which Freud's nephew had scribbled something like "If this is gonna work, boys, we gotta get the archbishop on board, and pronto," and bring it to her best friend in Our Lady's Guild House so that she could give it to the consul, who would pass it directly to President Arbenz, maybe in time to save the day? Doesn't seem so. At any rate, the day was never saved. Questioning Mamita [the author's mother] about the coup had turned out to be futile. If only I'd thought to ask her about it years ago. If only.

The speculation is even more compelling when the author reveals that his mother knew the ambassador, Cabot Lodge, and the upper-crust Bostonian "Brahmins" whom United Fruit Company employed.

This powerful book provides additional insights into the author's previous works. As *Publishers Weekly* correctly enthused: "Captivating...Goldman's direct, intimate writing alone is worth the price of admission." And *Kirkus's* starred review joined in with: "The warmth and humanity of Goldman's storytelling are impossible to resist."

A friend and fellow author, Tom Miller, an acclaimed travel writer (*The Panama Hat Trail*, among many), has held Goldman in high regard for years. Miller revealed that one of Goldman's essays was included in his compelling anthology of accomplished Latinos and their lessons about learning English and learning about life. Goldman's piece is entitled "Ghost Boy" and sheds light on what he refers to as his "binational" identification.

Goldman reveals that he spoke fluent Spanish as a four-year-old, but by the time he reached college, he only spoke English:

> *The little boy who at some point must have been able to speak both had been cleaved in two: one who spoke English and the other – vanished! A permanent absence. I was his ghost, and he was mine. In a sense, I've spent the last three decades, during which I've lived as much in Latin America as in the United States as if on a mission to bring those two boys together.*

The author tells of the pressure from school administrators in Boston to speak only English, "What kind of country produces educators who think it necessary to exorcize foreign languages and accents from little children?" he reflects on a Cuban writer friend's challenge of finding an adequate translator for his novel. "Wasn't the United States the richest, most powerful nation on Earth? Then how could it have such incompetent professional literary translators?" He pondered that question and told his Cuban friend, "It's because we're the nation we are, so rich and powerful, that we have such incompetent translators." He warns of the consequences of this reality: "A country that speaks to the world only in its language and describes reality to itself only in its own usage will be able to convince itself of anything."

Goldman would overcome this limitation after covering Central America's wars in the 1980s and 1990s as a freelance journalist:

I'm a fairly fluent Spanish speaker again, just like when I was four. For years, my mother and I have spoken only Spanish to each other. To get my Spanish back took a long time and an enormous commitment. To borrow a certain literary metaphor, it was like constructing my garden of forking paths that I can follow back into the past, to a place where that lost boy and I were never separated, and forward into a familiar landscape where two separate countries comprise one.

Goldman's book, **The Art of Political Murder**, published in 2007, reflects the fruits of his hard work and insights informed by his coverage of the wars in Central America in the 1980s as a contributing editor for *Harper's Magazine*. Initially, Goldman thought he would write "a short book on the Bishop Gerardi murder case, a work of journalism," but it turned out to be so much more. It represented an almost surreal detective story that opened the door into the Latin American reality of state-sponsored assassinations and organized crime.

The book is a non-fiction account of the assassination of Guatemalan Catholic Bishop Juan Jose Gerardi Conedera in 1998 by the Guatemalan military, an expansion of an article he wrote for *The New Yorker*. Goldman underwent seven years of painstaking and often dangerous investigative digging for the book. Rachel Kushner, who interviewed Goldman for Lit Hub, characterized the author as "a brave and storied journalist who has risked his life to speak truth to power - super gonzo."

Bishop Gerardi, Guatemala's leading human rights activist, was bludgeoned to death in his garage, only a few hundred feet from the government's most sophisticated security units and surveillance apparatus. This occurred only two days after a groundbreaking church-sponsored report was released, implicating the military in the murders and disappearances of some 200,000 civilians.

Goldman tells how the Catholic Church formed an investigative team of secular young men in their twenties known as *"Los Intocables"* [The Untouchables]. The murder was known in the tabloids as "The Crime of the Century." Corruption was apparent at all levels: the expected lack of interest of police investigators and the inability of the existing legal system to deal with the crime. In what would be his first non-fiction book, Goldman managed to reach and interview witnesses that no other reporter or authority could access; he witnessed first-hand some of the crucial developments in the case unfolding before him.

Goldman's investigation reveals the involvement of several United States administrations in creating some of the circumstances that led to the bloody Civil War. They resulted from a coup engineered by the CIA in 1954 against Jacobo Arbenz, only the second democratically elected president in Guatemala's history. This reality was confirmed with a remarkable apology by President Bill Clinton on a visit to Guatemala in 1999, according to a passage in ***The Art of Political Murder.*** When sitting next to stone-faced President Alvaro Arzu, he said: "It is important that I state clearly that support for military forces or intelligence units that engaged in violent and widespread repression of the kind described in the report was wrong...and the United States must not repeat that mistake."

Goldman takes the reader through Guatemala's byzantine legal system and describes the constant threats against judges and witnesses (several of whom had to leave the country, fearing for their lives). Many of the rulings on the case were flawed; for example, in the Fourth Court of Appeals, where the appellate judges did not even request vital witness records.

Finally, in January 2006, the author received confirmation by email that the Supreme Court had upheld the convictions and thirty-year sentences for several of the perpetrators. At hearing the news, Goldman felt astonished, yet relieved. However, attempts to limit and delay the convictions continued until April 2007, when a new judge took over as President of the Constitutional Court. Not until April 25th

- the day before the ninth anniversary of the murder of Bishop Gerardi - did the Public Ministry give notification that the guilty verdicts against the Limas (military officers who planned the assassination) and Father Mario Orantes (a Catholic priest who was complicit in the murder) had finally been upheld. Only after the convictions were upheld did Goldman feel he could advance with *The Art of Political Murder.*

In an interview for Lit Hub, the author describes why his perspective is unique:

> *The protagonists of that historic catastrophe are Central Americans; they're the ones who lived and overwhelmingly gave their lives, who survived and endured even if gringos were responsible for so much of that nightmare. You'll notice, if you read Bolaño or Castellanos Moya, that they never commit the gaucherie, if I can call it that, of explicitly blaming the U.S. for the violent political catastrophes depicted in some of their novels, even though, of course they know what happened. They're "our" stories. But an American like Deborah Eisenberg is writing for an American audience; she's performing a brilliantly subtle and deeply felt sort of assault on conscience and obliviousness. An essentially binational writer like me is pulled in both directions.*

After several years of reading and reviewing Goldman's books, I've been increasingly impressed by his considerable talents as a writer and his unique insights into the realities of Guatemala and Central America. I recently learned from an author friend that, at one point, Goldman had been considered for a MacArthur "Genius Grant." However, the real impact and legacy of the author is most evident in the many ways people have tried to reproduce his work for an ever-growing audience.

The Art of Political Murder (based on Goldman's book), premiered late last year and has been nominated for an Emmy. The documentary clarifies a complex storyline that probes multiple layers of the reality of power and corruption in Guatemala. The film, produced by George Clooney and Grant Heslov, includes dramatic interviews with key witnesses, investigators, and prosecutors.

We learn about the theories of who killed the bishop and why. Among these theories are organized crime, drug traffickers, and church thieves; it was even proposed that it was a crime of passion. Not only does the film chronicle the police investigation, but it also closely follows its internal dynamics. It explores crime and its aftermath - including governmental and military corruption and more attempted violence.

Most of the film focuses on what happened after the murder: a botched crime scene, numerous theories, citizen protests, and a high-profile trial. It's the story behind the story. The bishop was an outspoken activist for the Maya people and was beloved by many. The revelations about the police investigation leave you wondering what kind of government would issue a state-sponsored hit on a religious leader of the people.

But the bombshell in the courtroom was a homeless witness, Chantax, who revealed that he wasn't actually homeless; instead, he was an undercover informant tasked by military intelligence with spying on Bishop Gerardi. Moreover, on the fateful night in question, he had been recruited by three army officers to help with the crime. The trio received thirty years behind bars, while Father Mario Orantes got twenty.

After you view the film, check out the conversation on YouTube hosted by Director Paul Taylor with author Francisco Goldman, investigator Arturo Aguilar, and Guatemalan journalist Claudia Méndez Arriaza. They talk about the making of the film, the impact of Bishop Gerardi's murder, and updates surrounding the case.

When asked what his great takeaway from the film is, Goldman reflects on how justice and democracy must be fought for. People often talk in platitudes about "fighting for justice," but it takes the little guy, the common person in the street like the "homeless" witness, Chantax, to step up and speak truth to power. The small guy needs to "step up and take a risk and have the courage" to fight back when justice and democratic rule are under attack. He points to the principal investigator and the Guatemalan journalist as the real heroes, as they are still in Guatemala, as possible targets for reprisal.

When questioned about the ongoing efforts to bring about justice and transparency in Guatemala, Goldman points out that for progress to be made, local judicial institutions need support from their international counterparts. Without outside support, intimidation and violence will continue to stifle real justice. According to Goldman, the day in 2015 when ex-general President Otto Perez Molina went from the presidency to prison was one of the great triumphs in combating corruption. But he goes on to say that when former Guatemalan President Jimmy Morales and former President Trump tried to destroy the foundations of the justice system in their respective countries, the battle was not over.

The HBO production also produced a historical timeline for those not familiar with the history of Guatemala, the impact of the U.S., and the circumstances leading up to the tragic assassination of human rights activist Bishop Gerardi.

The Art of Political Murder Timeline

Although the MacArthur "Genius" award never materialized, Goldman did receive a 2017 Barnes & Noble Writers for Writers Prize and PEN Mexico's 2017 Award for Journalistic and Literary Excellence. Also, he has been a Guggenheim Fellow, a Cullman Center Fellow at the NY Public Library, a Berlin Fellow at the American Academy of Arts, and a member of the American Academy of Arts and Sciences. In addition to his five novels and two non-fiction books, Goldman has written for *The New Yorker, The New York Times Magazine, Harper's, The Believer,* and many other publications. He directs the Aura Estrada Prize.

Recently, I asked Goldman to be interviewed for a documentary I am co-producing, **Trouble in the Highlands**. Many of the stories will be narrated by, and understood, through the eyes and perspective of Guatemalan Indigenous leaders. Goldman will be part of a diverse team that includes prominent Indigenous academics and activists, an award-winning journalist and media producer, a former NGO (non-government organization) executive/writer, and a seasoned videographer/director.

> *"I think everything you are, everything that engages you, eventually comes to bear on the novel you write. I think the creative energy in novel writing, obviously, comes from tension. From trying to fuse. From trying to make coherent disparate things that might not at all seem to belong together within a narrative."*
> — *Francisco Goldman*

Chapter 7

TRAVELING THROUGH THE LAND OF THE ETERNAL SPRING, A LITERARY JOURNEY

Books have always been an essential part of my life. In the Peace Corps, volunteers were given a trunk of books, including works of Dostoyevsky, Tolstoy, and Tolkien, but none on Guatemala. So, when I discovered that Guatemala had a Nobel Literature Laureate, I read Miguel Angel Asturias's novel, **The President** (El Señor Presidente).

Although it was published before I was born, its relevance persists, as it portrays the damaging psychological impact of a totalitarian government and the brutality it will exercise to maintain power - a phenomenon all too real to Guatemalans today.

The dictator depicted in the novel is Guatemalan President Manuel Estrada Cabrera (1898-1920). As a young law student, the author started writing the book in the 1920s. However, it wasn't finished until thirteen years later in Mexico due to the strict censorship policies of the Guatemalan dictatorial government.

The author draws from experience as a journalist writing about repressive conditions, as reflected in this passage about the plight of political prisoners: "Two hours of light, twenty-two hours of utter darkness, one tin of soup and one of excrement, thirst in summer, floods in winter; that was life in the underground cells."

One of the things that attracted me to Asturias' works was his interest in the Maya Indigenous population, its culture, myths and legends, its plight, and how all those factors influenced his writing style and subject matter. His father was a judge who clashed with the dictatorship of Manuel Estrada Cabrera, and he was forced to send his family to their grandparents in the town of Salamá, which is close to where I met my wife.

This would be the author's initial contact with Guatemala's Indigenous groups, and his nanny, a young Indigenous woman, who told him stories of their myths and legends, which influenced his works. His university thesis was "The Social Problem of the Indian." He later studied ethnology at the University of Paris. His deep concern for the Maya culture led to a forty-year project to translate the Maya sacred text, the **Popol Vuh**, into Spanish. It also inspired his second novel, **Men of Maiz**, perhaps his masterpiece, written as a myth that contrasts traditional Maya customs and beliefs with outside forces pushing, often brutally, for modernization on their terms.

Following the Second World War, the United States increased its presence in Latin America, and companies like the United Fruit Company manipulated politicians and exploited land and Guatemalan workers. In **The Green Pope**, the second book in his **The Banana Trilogy,** the founder of United Fruit explains that men should be ruled by force or left alone. "They're governed to make them develop, the way children are punished for their good, for their future development."

The consequence of this force played out along the waters of the Montagua River, where the flood of dead bodies floated out to sea. **The Green Pope**, coincidentally, was published in 1954, the same year the reformist government of Jacobo Arbenz, which Asturias strongly supported, was overthrown by a CIA-led coup. Asturias was expelled by the government and fled to Argentina.

Mario Vargas Llosa, a Peruvian author and a Nobel Prize for Literature Laureate, also wrote a book, **Harsh Times**, about the overthrow of the Arbenz government, perhaps the most seminal event in Guatemalan history.

The author does a laudable job researching the circumstances and enhances an appreciation of reality through the fictional characters he develops. The dialogue between the Guatemalan president and the U.S. ambassador reveals the power dynamics that existed between the two countries, starting with the U.S. ambassador:

> *"Forty communist members of your government," the ambassador said with extremely undiplomatic curtness. "I am asking you in the name of the United States to remove them from their posts immediately as infiltrators in the service of a foreign power working against the interests of Guatemala."*

The Guatemalan president glanced at the list, which included some good friends, close collaborators, and a few self-declared leftists, many no more communist than he was. To which the president says, "We're starting off on the wrong foot, Ambassador. You've been badly informed..." It ends with, "Have you forgotten that Guatemala is a sovereign nation and that you are an ambassador, not a viceroy or proconsul?"

The press played an important role, along with the U.S. government, in protecting United Fruit against an imaginary "Red Threat," as articulated by the head of United Fruit: "What threat? The same one I have just told you Guatemala doesn't represent: the Soviet Trojan horse sneaking through to U.S.A.'s back door."

According to the author, the consequences of this debacle made Guatemala "a frantic country," gripped by a ruinous and wholly unnecessary antipathy towards something that never threatened and is soon "racing backward toward tribalism and absurdity."

PART II

THE YIN & YANG OF TRAVEL

Chapter 8

MY LIFE IN THE LAND OF THE ETERNAL SPRING: THE COFFEE PLANTATION

Four-year-old Michelle with Airedale puppy at her great-grandfather's coffee plantation

Several fellow writers asked why I'm so passionate about Guatemala and its people. The answer is simple. As a young man out of college, I lived in a Guatemalan village as a Peace Corps volunteer. I also married a Guatemalan, Ligia, who has been my life partner for over forty-eight years. My children were all born in Guatemala. So, you might say Guatemala is in my blood. And the importance of Guatemala to us has become more apparent as a growing number of Central Americans are fleeing their communities in the hopes of a better life here.

I arrived in the highlands of Guatemala as a Peace Corps volunteer in the early '70s, and as I describe in my book, ***Different Latitudes: My Life in the Peace Corps and Beyond,*** a third of my life takes place there. Each morning at dawn in the village of Calapté, I'd stroll over to a nearby family's home for breakfast, which cost me twenty-five cents.

One morning, I awoke with a horrendous stomach cramp; I was sweating profusely and only semi-conscious. I didn't have the strength to get out of bed, let alone walk the forty-five minutes uphill to the only daily bus that passed. The Peace Corps staff had assured me that if I ever got ill or had an accident, I'd be medevacked in a helicopter, which sounded good at the time, until I realized that the telegraph system was down and the only phone in the community didn't work. I was up the proverbial creek.

Fortunately, when I didn't turn up for breakfast, Doña Martha, who was like a second mother, came looking for me with several friends, found me in bed in a daze, and gave me a series of herbal drinks and indigenous wisdom. These three women saved my life, and within three days, I was hiking up the hill to catch the bus to the Peace Corps headquarters in Guatemala City.

My medical ordeal was too risky to remain in such a remote village, so the Peace Corps staff sent me to San Jeronimo, closer to communication and potential evacuation roads. Shortly after my arrival, my eyes locked on a strawberry-blond girl who, it turned out, was visiting her father's small horse ranch.

I was smitten at first sight, but like a dumb gringo, I wasn't sure how to proceed with this pretty girl. A Guatemalan friend from my new village made the introduction: her name was Ligia, and she agreed to have coffee with me.

"So, where did you go to school?" I wanted to find out if she'd gotten through high school.

"Well, actually, I have several degrees. One is a teaching certificate, and the other is a degree in agricultural engineering from the University of San Carlos."

Then I asked a trick question about what she does in her spare time, thinking she hung around her house. "Oh, I love drama and have been involved in the university theater. Carmina Burana is by far my favorite play."

Carmina who? I thought. I was in over my head, but I didn't let that stop me, and within five months, we were married. We often visited her grandfather's coffee plantation, "San Francisco Miramar," on the side of the volcano, Atitlán.

On one of those visits over Christmas, I came across my five-year-old daughter, Michelle, in the "Big House," hugging her gift, an Airedale puppy. A dozen small children behind her were pushed up against the screen door. Although I couldn't distinguish their faces, these were the plantation workers' children who stood dressed in simple cotton shirts, jeans, and flip-flops, silently peering into the room filled with unopened gifts and an ornate Christmas tree.

They were so cute, inquisitive, and innocent, yet none dared open the door and enter. I kissed my daughter on the forehead and continued through the room to a porch on the far side of the "Big House," where I shared the encounter with my Guatemalan wife, Ligia.

As we both gazed up the side of the volcano and took in the sweet aroma of the coffee blooms, I informed my wife that my calling would be to assure that children of the humblest families might receive a decent education and aspire to a career of their choice.

Chapter 9

MY SADDEST PLEASURES: TAKING DONORS TO THE FAR REACHES OF THE WORLD

TRAVEL IS FATAL TO PREJUDICE, BIGOTRY, AND NARROW-MINDEDNESS, AND MANY OF OUR PEOPLE NEED IT SORELY ON THESE ACCOUNTS. BROAD, WHOLESOME, CHARITABLE VIEWS OF MEN AND THINGS CANNOT BE ACQUIRED BY VEGETATING IN ONE LITTLE CORNER OF THE EARTH ALL ONE'S LIFETIME. —MARK TWAIN, THE INNOCENTS ABROAD

Food for the Hungry staff and board members waiting for our small plane in Nebaj, Quiche

In my late forties, as a senior director of Food for the Hungry (FHI), I led several groups of child sponsors, plus their children in some cases, and Foundation board members, to the departments of Quiché and Alta Verapaz in Guatemala. Twenty years before these tours, I had helped set up a local Indigenous foundation in San Andrés Sajcabajá in Quiché. I knew the area had some of the most horrendous roads winding through the Cuchumatane mountains.

Large trucks hauled workers to the south coast during the rainy season to harvest coffee. They would put chains on the back four tires to enhance traction, but the chains and the weight of the trucks destroyed the roads. I also knew the health dangers of traveling to this part of Guatemala. We almost lost our middle daughter after she contracted amoebas while living with us on a project farm I had helped establish.

Since the 1980s, the area was also the center of thirteen years of violence, with the local Ixil-speaking Indigenous population caught between leftist guerrillas and right-wing death squads. Some 15,000 had been killed, and thousands more displaced. I came across drawings of FHI-sponsored children, which depicted helicopters and planes dropping napalm and bombs on their communities. This happened, and it traumatized the local population, especially children.

This was not an area for casual tourists, but FHI's programs were excellent and we were all impressed by the dedication of the staff who coordinated our visits. At no point did we ever feel we might be in danger. After many years of doing this, I understood the importance of including children on these tours, as they represented the next generation of philanthropists. Also, many parents wanted to expose their children to how others lived worldwide.

So, in March of 1997, I took Bill Williams and two of his daughters, fifteen-year-old Sarah and eight-year-old Emily, to Guatemala. My associate, John Scola, also invited John and Jeanette Tornquist from Illinois, generous and committed supporters. We flew on two small Cessna planes from Guatemala City to Santa Maria Nebaj in the Ixil Triangle of the Department of Quiché.

When we arrived, a Hunger Corps volunteer, Jodi Johnson, provided a program overview. The Hunger Corps was like a Christian Peace Corps organized by FHI. Volunteers made a two-year commitment. After Jodi's program overview and visits to water projects close by, it had clouded over, and

I realized the two planes would not be returning due to inclement weather, a frequent occurrence.

I often traveled in small planes to the San Andres Sacatepéquez area, which is close by, when I worked there years before, and sometimes I had to wait over a week until the clouds parted long enough for the pilots to return. But this timeline wouldn't work for donors who had other plans, so I worked with our local staff to identify other transportation options and finally commandeered an old "chicken" bus (a former school bus painted with local scenes) and a driver, and our little band headed out over a dusty, bumpy road from Nebaj through Uspantán next to the Chixoy River, and eventually to our destination, Cobán, the departmental capital of Alta Verapaz. We had to leave the windows down because the bus had no air conditioning, allowing a steady stream of dust to enter. Seven hours later, covered in a fine layer of dust, shaken up, and in a daze, we finally reached Cobán.

After a quick orientation in Cobán from Patricia Cuba, the Country Director for FHI, we headed out in Land Cruisers to the community of Chiguorrán, where FHI supported a local school program. Classes were taught in the Mayan language of Poqomchi. Little Emily distributed balloons during recess and played with the students about her age. Then, the Tornquists and Emily showed the children how to blow bubbles. They all laughed and had a great time together. The language barrier didn't seem to be an issue.

FHI pairs up a U.S. sponsor, who pays $21 a month to provide support such as education and food to a child in a program country equivalent to Guatemala. The trip's highlight was the Williamses' encounter with the child they sponsored, Carmela. We hiked twenty minutes from the vehicle to Carmela's house, which was traditional for the area: a thatch-roofed kitchen in the back and a wood plank dwelling in the front. Firewood was piled up on the front porch. Several coffee and fruit trees, including bananas, surrounded the house. The animals, chickens, and piglets were kept behind the kitchen area. The house had a cement floor, and plastic sheets separated the interior into rooms.

Initially, Carmela's parents couldn't find her because she was hiding in the cornfield until the foreigners (us) left. When her father finally brought her to us, she wore a simple white blouse and a blue skirt with plastic sandals on her feet. She was shorter than Emily's shoulder, although she was probably the same age. I took a picture of Bill with the two girls and another with Carmela and her sister. I didn't see any windows in their house, which would explain why it seemed so dark inside, even during the day.

Carmela's father showed us around, and we sat on the front porch. Sarah and Emily began asking how they lived: What do you grow? Why doesn't the kitchen have a chimney? How does Carmela get to school? (Walking one and a half hours per day). Where will Carmela go after she graduates from the local school? What do you eat for dinner? Where's the bathroom? What was the round white structure in the back? (The girls could see the traditional steam bath that uses hot rocks and water to clean off, like our shower.) Carmela and her father responded to these questions and asked a few of their own, like where did Sarah and Emily live? Eventually, we had to say our goodbyes, and we brought the Williamses back to Cobán.

Despite the change in flight plans, rough roads, and cloudy, very long days, everyone in the group survived. They had seen an isolated part of the country, which wasn't that different from other parts of Guatemala, and they had met a local family up close and personal. None would be the same after this experience, and the Williams children would later become serious philanthropists, just like their father. Regarding Carmela, that's more difficult to say, as the sponsorship program discontinues when the children graduate from primary school, so FHI often loses track of their whereabouts.

Obviously, after fifty years on the road, much of it in and around Guatemala, I am still capable of some real travel gaffes. And yet, we're almost at our best and learn the most when we miscalculate and must depend on the locals (and our wits) to figure a way out of a mess. And Theroux's quip proved so true. "Travel is the saddest of pleasures as it gave me eyes," no matter one's age. And yes, Moritz Thomsen was right: "Life is a bitch, and then you die," but neither of us would have had it any other way.

Chapter 10

Trekking Through Guatemala with Kids

Lake Atitlan

After almost twenty-five years of marriage and three children born in Guatemala, my Guatemalan wife and I realized it was time to reintroduce them back to their native land. Our middle daughter, Nicolle, hadn't been back for nearly twenty-five years, and her significant other, Ed, had never been there. Our son, John, hadn't been back for twenty years. Michelle, our oldest daughter, also hadn't been back to Guatemala for many years, but had her hands full with five children. Nicolle and John, however, were available, so in 2013, we headed to Guatemala together.

Traveling in Guatemala had changed radically since I was kicking around the highlands in the early 1970s in the brightly painted "chicken" buses. When I applied for a position as Peace Corps Guatemala Country Director several years before our trip, I was informed that Peace Corps Volunteers were not even allowed into Guatemala City, the capital, unless in an official van, and some had curfews starting at 6:00 p.m. Local robberies and drug-related incidents had put volunteers at serious risk.

This was not "my" Peace Corps, so past experiences traveling with Ligia had forced me to update my Yin & Yang Travel List radically, starting with my propensity to base all decisions on what is cheapest. To get everyone ready, I recommended they read ***The Guatemala Reader: History, Culture, Politics***, as it provides the most extensive source of background information about the country's culture and history. For my part, the first thing I did was connect with our old friend, Chati, manager of the Hotel Tolimán in San Lucas Tolimán, Guatemala, who would arrange a driver with a van to get us around.

Conrado was waiting for us at the Aurora International Airport in Guatemala City and we headed for one of the most beautiful lakes in the world, Lake Atitlán, via the south coast route through Escuintla. Although Guatemala City is filled with fascinating sights, its organization, cleanliness, and some aspects of security have improved over the years, it's still a big, expensive city, so I decided to leave it for the end of our trip.

After leaving the airport, we zipped down the paved highway headed for the south coast, past endless dark green sugar cane plantations and innumerable Cebu cattle grazing on grass-covered hills, oblivious to the damp, sticky, hot air of the coast. Occasionally, we'd pass under huge majestic Ceiba trees. Gradually, we began gaining altitude through Patulul, which was not far from the coffee and cardamom plantation where I initially courted Ligia, and her family-owned plantation (San Francisco Miramar), which was situated at the base of the majestic volcano Atitlán.

As we gained altitude, we turned off the air conditioning and opened the windows. A cool breeze entered the van. Ligia and I began telling stories of how we rode horses up the back side of the plantation into the "*cafetal*" during the Easter holiday when the hills were covered with white flowers and the sweet perfume smell engulfed us.

Our collective breath was taken as we climbed the Sierra Madre Mountain range and caught our first glimpse of Lake Atitlán. German explorer and naturalist Alexander von Humboldt called it "the most beautiful lake in the world." Atitlán, the deepest lake in Central America, sits among the mountains and is bordered by three volcanoes and twelve Maya villages, some named after the apostles. The Maya people here are predominantly Tz'utujil and Kaqchikel, and still wear their colorful traditional attire.

The Hotel Tolimán was on the side of the towering volcano Tolimán and faced the lake. We would start each day on the second-floor patio with a traditional Guatemalan breakfast of eggs with black beans and sour cream, fried plantains, papaya with a piece of lemon, cantaloupe, and, of course, a strong cup of Guatemalan Arabic coffee fresh off the slopes of one of the volcanoes. Ligia and I would finish our coffee from the balcony as the kids pushed their kayaks onto the lake below.

Conrado was from the area and owned his van. He told us about the celebration of Corpus Cristi in the community of Patzún, known by few foreign tourists, but where over 20,000 locals came to town. When we arrived in Patzún, the streets were covered with colorful sawdust carpets like those filling La Antigua's streets during Easter Week. The local women add to the collage of colors with their *huipils* (hand-woven brightly colored red blouses woven in strips with native dyes).

As we entered the middle of town, which overlooked the cathedral, many locals were leaving Catholic Mass, praying and singing as they walked over the sawdust carpets lining the streets. The Eucharist, known as the Blessed Sacrament, was placed in a monstrance and held aloft by a clergy member. Still, soon, he seemed intermingled with several local Maya priests carrying statues and wearing costumes. Eventually, the procession returned to the church where Benediction took place. As we left, my daughter reflected, "What an amazing cultural mix between the Maya groups and the Catholic church!"

The next day, we wound our way through the Sierra Madre Mountains to the Maya town of Chichicastenango, where the Sierra Madres meet the Sierra de Chaucús at more than 6,000 feet. Chichi (as it is often called in Guatemala) is the spiritual center of the K'iche Maya. It includes the iconic, four-hundred-year-old "Catedral Santo Tomás," built atop a pre-Columbian temple platform where Maya priests still burn incense and candles as part of their rituals. Each of the eighteen steps leading up to the church stands for one month of the Maya calendar and is covered with flowers, food, and other things sold at the market next to the church.

The market is filled with colorful Maya handicrafts - the wooden masks have been our weakness over the years, and we just had to add them to our collection. The masks are used in traditional dances like the Dance of the Conquest. Pottery, condiments, medicinal plants, pom, and copal (traditional incense that is constantly burning on the steps), *cal* (limestones used for preparing tortillas), pigs, chickens, and machetes round out the collection of items on display. Although my wife and children speak fluent Spanish and could bargain with the local merchants, I reminded them not to negotiate the price down too hard, though at the same time, I didn't want to pay the highest "tourist" price for our purchases.

Later, we hiked out of town to the Cofradia of Pascual Abaj, an ancient carved stone revered by the locals, where Maya priests perform different rituals. The writing on the stone reportedly records the activities of a deity of the K'iche Maya god named Tohil (Fate). We didn't take any photos out of respect for the local priests. When we finally reached the top of the hill, the air was filled with the smell of copal as the priests added local items to the fire they worked and prayed over.

I passed on the cheapest pension in Chichi in favor of the venerable Hotel Santo Tomás, designed like a colonial convent. That evening in the hotel we had dinner sitting next to the fireplace, which generated a warm glow that permeated the entire dining area. During dinner, we enjoyed several Gallo beers, the local favorite. Modelo is the other excellent local beer, but none could compare with my choice of years ago, when Cabro was sold in two-liter bottles and provided the best excuse to sit down and chat with some of the local men. After dinner, the girls had to stop at the gift shop before leaving. There, they found an excellent book on the German influence on the coffee culture, *The History of Coffee in Guatemala*, by Regina Wagner, filled with historic black and white photos and maps of the coffee-producing areas.

The next day, we returned to Lake Atitlán. On our last evening at the Hotel Tolimán, a cold mist hung over the area, making the fireplace in our room the perfect place to warm up and discuss the next day's plans. The following morning, our van climbed the steep roads out of the lake area, then headed down the Pan-American Highway (highway in name only) bound for the former colonial capital of Guatemala, La Antigua, a UNESCO World Heritage site. In Antigua, cobblestone streets and streetscapes of pastel façades unfold beneath the gaze of three imposing volcanoes. The town is filled with colonial buildings, often next to well-restored ruins from the sixteenth century.

I took the family to the dining area of La Posada de Don Rodrigo, as it has the most spectacular open courtyard in town. It is filled with wrought iron, bright-colored bougainvillea and other flowers, tinkling fountains, and, of course, the iconic *marimba* being played the entire time. Local women in their traditional Maya dresses make the tortillas as you wait. Most of us ordered the *plato típico*, which includes a tender piece of *carne a la parrilla* (grilled meat), black beans, rice, *chirmol* (a roasted tomato-spearmint-based sauce), avocado, cooked plantains with sour cream, sausages, and as many corn tortillas as you could possibly eat. All the servers wore traditional Maya clothing, and some even pulled a few of us away from the table to dance the *el son*, a traditional Maya waltz-like dance.

After dinner, we strolled under the iconic Santa Catalina Arch and headed down the cobblestone street towards the historic baroque church La Merced. Its yellow and white colors make it unique in town and, quite possibly, the whole country. After a long day sightseeing, we stopped at one of the many local watering holes and had a few Gallos while watching Peru and Panama play a regional soccer game.

The next day, the kids rented bicycles and eventually made it to the large cross on top of the high hill (Cerro de la Cruz), which faces the iconic Volcán de Agua in one direction and, in the other, offers a spectacular view of the historic colonial town.

With two of our three children in-country, it seemed like a great time to host a family reunion! We decided to host it at Las Orquideas, a restored hacienda on the highway between Guatemala City and La Antigua. We had grilled beef, rice, black beans, avocados, and lots of Gallo beer. Ligia put together a collage of photos of our children at the entrance of the eating area, since many of their cousins hadn't seen them in over twenty years, and everyone seemed to have grown up!

Most of Ligia's family was from Guatemala City. Still, on her father's side, they had to come from San Jerónimo in Baja Verapaz, where I met Ligia as a Peace Corps volunteer all those years ago. My favorite image of the event was when three generations of teachers - Christi (who taught for sixty years), her daughter Christabel (fifty years), and Ligia (who has taught for over forty years) huddled together, commis- erating. Close to one hundred people attended the reunion, making it almost the same number who had participated in our wedding so many years ago, albeit I was told that only the "immediate" family would come.

After many hours of embraces and hugs with family members (some almost forgotten), the kids headed off together to an old bar in the middle of town. Several of the children had taken similar paths in life. The son of Ligia's cousin became a lawyer, as did our son, John. Ligia's niece, Vera María, worked for an international development group, and our daughter, Nicolle, has been working for the International Rescue Committee for fifteen years.

Nicolle expressed a real nostalgia for her native country, culture, and family that developed toward the end of our trip. She hadn't stayed in touch with her cousins, who were only children when we left, but she was impressed that these "familiar strangers" had grown into "fantastic adults." Not only did she hold a similar career path to Vera Maria, but they also had much in common regarding their love of travel and music.

She went on to reflect:

> *"These feelings were bittersweet because, while I appreciated rekindling those connections, it left me wishing I had been there to grow up with them. I get the sense that we would have made great musical discoveries together, attended more than a few protests and rallies as cousins, and would have become great friends. The beautiful thing is that we will always have each other in our lives, and there will be future chances when our paths might cross again. But there is a bittersweet nostalgia of what you've missed over the thirty years of being away."*

Today, our three children have provided eight grandchildren, which will necessitate our updating the Yin & Yang Travel List for the next generation to reconnect with their Guatemalan roots.

Chapter 11

TSCHIFFELY'S EPIC EQUESTRIAN RIDE: OVER THE ANDES TO GUATEMALA

Tshiffely with his two criolla horses

Tschiffely's Ride tells the story of one of the most incredible horse rides ever. A.F. Tschiffely's 10,000-mile journey through Latin America over a three-year period from 1925 to 1928 made him one of the most influential equestrian travel writers of his day.

My interest in his journey was piqued by my 15,000-mile, eleven-country trip, going from Guatemala to Southern Chile and back again over a five-month period, forty-five years after Tschiffely's trip. He and I passed through many of the same out-of-the-way places. Further, my trip was also by land, my modes of transportation being bus, truck, train, and an occasional taxi, with one exception: a plane ride from Panama to Colombia (the author circumvented this portion of his trip in a ferry).

Tschiffely was thirty years old at the outset of his journey and had been the headmaster of a high school in Buenos Aires, Argentina for several years. As he explains in his book, although he enjoyed his work, he wanted a change, some variety, and adventure: "I was young and fit; the idea of this journey had been in my ear for years, and finally, I determined to make the attempt."

Some of the newspapers in Buenos Aires deemed his announced trip as "impossible" and "absurd," yet he was not deterred. For his journey, Tschiffely decided on two Creole horses, descendants of horses brought to Argentina in 1535 by the founder of Buenos Aires, Don Pedro Mendoza. So, the fitness and resilience of his mounts were amply proven.

Almost as soon as Tschiffely headed north out of Buenos Aires, he started passing isolated communities, one of which was Santiago del Estero. There, he realized that the dark thundercloud he saw coming his way was, in fact, an "invasion of locusts," which formed a thick carpet. "Every cactus plant and shrub was overhung with a grey mass...." It was a warning of additional surprises and adventures to come.

One of his biggest challenges was trying to get directions from the local population wherever: "It is no use asking these people the way, for they have only one answer and will invariably reply, "sige derecho no mas" (just go straight ahead), although the trail may wind and twist though a regular labyrinth of deep canyons and valleys."

Eventually, Tschiffely and his two steeds would make their way to the Altiplano area of South America, and the silver-mining town of Potosí, Bolivia, one of the highest cities in the world. This portion of his book brought back personal memories of some severe altitude sickness at over 13,000 feet. Tschiffely often shared the local history of the places he visited, and, in this case, the horrors of early Spanish Colonial days. Their principal mine on the iconic Cerro Rico was called *Socabon*. The Spanish coat of arms was carved into the rocks over the entrance where an "estimated 20,000 Indians were driven into the darkness of this mine, and none who entered there ever saw daylight again."

Another situation that evoked personal memories occurred in the Andes Mountains around Ayacucho, Peru, where "Landslides and swollen rivers made it impossible to follow the road and compelled me to make a large detour over the mountains to the west." In my case, forty-five years later, another landslide in the same area forced me to make a long detour on my way to Chile. On my return trip to Ayacucho, I learned that the same road had still not been cleared, almost three months and six countries later, resulting in "Plan C" to reach Lima.

The author's detour was more harrowing, as he was forced to cross a "wild river" over a bridge, which was "like a long, thin rope, wire and fiber held the rickety structure together. The floor was made of sticks laid crosswise and covered with some coarse fiber matting to give a foothold and to prevent slipping that would inevitably prove fatal." This included walking across with his horses. His weight "shook the bridge so much that I had to catch hold of the wires on the sides to keep my balance...Once we started upward after crossing the middle, even the horse seemed to realize that we had passed the worst part, for now he began to hurry toward safety."

As if this wasn't dangerous enough, the author tells of a "mysterious disease" in Peru known as *verruga*, which is usually fatal and manifests itself in great swellings or boils. "The local opinion varied as to its cause. Some said it was the water; others said it was in the air, while some blame insects." Fortunately, the author and his steeds were not struck down by this local malady.

Another situation I could identify with was crossing from Ecuador into Colombia over a natural bridge called Rumichaca (Quechua for stone bridge), where customs officers "wearing dirty clothes, stopped us and demanded to see my documents." But this is where our experiences differed, as I was usually harassed and delayed by heavily armed teenage guards looking for a bribe. Still, in Tschiffely's case, "they had been advised of my arrival and treated me with courtesy." Evidently, the author's embassy did an excellent job alerting local authorities of his pending arrival and was treated as an honored guest.

In Central America, Tschiffely spent significant time in Guatemala. One of the first places the author visited in Guatemala City was the famous relief map in Minerva Park, a place I have seen many times to get an idea of where some of the isolated villages I worked in were in relation to the rest of the country. "This map is made to a 1/10,000 scale horizontally and 1/2,000 vertically. It is made of concrete, and running water marks the rivers, lakes, and oceans." The nuance in Tschiffely's case was: "On my way back [to his hotel], the streetcar derailed, and the driver asked me to help him lift it back on the rails."
The author also encountered a darker side of Guatemalan history:

> *While in this city (Guatemala City) I saw a man kept in a dungeon below the San Francisco church for sixteen years. This happened during Cabrera's time. Food and water were lowered through a hole to the prisoners below, and those who died were hoisted out through the same opening.*

Fortunately, Tschiffely did not miss one of the more spectacular places in Guatemala, and possibly in all of Latin

America: "On reaching the summit of a high hill, after zigzagging higher and higher among the strong-smelling fir trees, I beheld, far below at our feet, Lake Atitlán. Its mirror-like surface of a deep blue reflected the surrounding mountains and the snow-white clouds that looked like huge airships. The lake is more than 4,500 feet above sea level and rivals anything Switzerland has to offer." Which he knew well, as he was born in Bern, Switzerland.

I also rode horses not far from this lake forty-five years later—on a coffee plantation on the Pacific side of one of the volcanoes next to the lake with my Guatemalan girlfriend, Ligia. We visited the Finca in the spring when the coffee plants were in full bloom and the aromatic smell wafted through the Cafetal. It was all very romantic at the time, and the horses were the best way of accessing some of the more isolated sections of the Cafetal where hundreds of seasonal pickers would soon be harvesting the lush red beans.

Tschiffely, on the other hand, took a short-cut from Lake Atitlán further into the Maya highlands and visited a village well known for its disdain for outsiders: "...this trail led over mountains and was rough in parts, and we had to pass through the village of Nahuala, which I had been warned to avoid. It is inhabited exclusively by Indians who will not tolerate the presence of a white man overnight. In Guatemala, as in most Central American countries, the sale of liquor is a state monopoly, but the Indians of Nahuala pay the government a certain sum each year for not sending alcohol into their district."

Tschiffely would be able to find places for him and his trusty steeds to stay on his trek through the highlands, as some of the better-off farmers had their horses and would ride or walk them to their fields and walk them back, usually with a harvest or firewood. The terrain was rugged, and the loads were heavy, making these working horses a very durable lot.

When I was in the Peace Corps, almost four decades after his trip, I needed a horse to access villages around San José Ojetenam, which was located deep in the highlands at

10,000 feet and from where I could see the two tallest points in Central America, the volcanoes of Tajumulco and Tacaná. But this challenging terrain meant the roads outside the town were impossible for vehicles to navigate much of the year.

I met my wife as she was riding a beautiful white horse through San Jerónimo, Baja Verapaz, where she was spending the weekend at her father's ranch. His favorite steed was "Zingaro," a black Arabian horse he taught to do the "Peruvian Paso" gait, an outward swinging leg action. When I finally returned from my five-month trek through Latin America, my wife and I headed to her father's ranch several months later with our daughter, who rode around on my lap on one of her grandfather's older, slower horses.

Tschifflely's next destination, Mexico, would be the most receptive country to the author, primarily because of his two mounts, Mancha and Gato, to whom he dedicates his book: "Mexicans are born horsemen and lovers of adventure and the open air, and therefore, our journey appealed to them. Without meaning to boast, I just add that, as a nation, they are the ones who best understood the significance, valued the merit of my undertaking, and showed their appreciation accordingly."

"Of all the banquets I have ever attended, the most brilliant and picturesque was given to me by the "Asociacion Nacional de Charros" (*Charros* are fancily dressed Mexican cowboys). It was appropriately given in the Don Quixote Hall in one of Mexico's finest hotels. The diplomatic corps was well represented, and all the participants who were *charros* wore the typical costumes of the different regions to which they belonged."

Upon his departure from Mexico City, Tschiffely reflects: "To my surprise, crowds of mounted *charros* were assembled near the stables, ready to accompany me out of town for some ten miles, where, after many embraces and fervent handshakes, I sadly watched them disappear behind a cloud of dust."

Tschiffely continued his journey to Washington where President Calvin Coolidge received him in the White House. Also, in D.C., he was honored by the National Geographic Society, which invited him to give a lecture.

After Tschiffely's Ride, he became a famous and successful author and moved to London, where he continued to write more books, one of which was a biography of his friend, Robert Cunninghame Graham, who wrote the preface for Tschiffely's Ride. In 1937, the author returned to South America and made another journey, this time by car, to the southern tip of the continent, recording his experiences among the natives and the changes brought on by modernity in ***This Way Southward*** (1940).

His book, *Tschiffely's Ride,* includes an excellent map, which plots this epic journey and includes various photographs. According to the *New York Times*: "It is pretty certain that the crafty Ulysses, Marco Polo, or the indomitable Drake would have been hard put to keep up with Tschiffely. This is a heroic book." This story touched me. It brought back many fond memories of my trek through Latin America, which started a life of travel and adventure.

PART III

CROSSING BORDERS

Chapter 12

THE FUTURE OF THE PEACE CORPS IN GUATEMALA

Anna Zauner received the evacuation notice at 10:00 p.m. on March 15th, 2020: Have your things packed and ready in an hour. "I was thirty minutes from home with nothing packed," according to Anna, "home" being the highlands of Guatemala where Anna was one of 165 Peace Corps Volunteers (PCVs) serving in the "Land of Eternal Spring." Due to the global outbreak of COVID-19, over 7,300 PCVs were being evacuated from sixty-one countries.

Departure for Anna was chaotic, with many "stops and starts." After saying goodbye to as many friends as possible in Santa Lucía Utatlán, Sololá, Anna headed to a hotel near the airport in Guatemala City to await a chartered flight to depart the following day. After a sleepless night, Anna and her fellow volunteers discovered that the flight had been canceled due to "restricted airspace." Restricted airspace! What did that mean? After U.S. embassy officials negotiated with the Guatemalan government, the volunteers - flanked by the embassy and police escorts - headed for the airport with sirens blaring and lights flashing, the multiple vehicle escort something right out of a Hollywood movie. Once the plane lifted off, there was a palatable sense of relief, and a few hours later, they touched down in Miami.

The first thing that occurred to Anna once she returned was that she was happy to be home, but: "What about the ones I left behind? When I told my host family in Guatemala and tried to explain through tears that I was hoping to come back but was unsure if I would be able to, they said to me, 'No tenga pena' (Don't worry), for the lack of goodbyes for leaving the community I pledged to serve for two years. The students I was teaching have been spending their time at home, leaving quiet soccer fields and classrooms bereft of laughter. I hope the lecture I gave on positive youth development through life skills will protect students in the future. There was so much more, which I did not get to address: substance abuse, reproductive health, and mental health, for starters."

Anna Zauner is one of a long line of Peace Corps Volunteers (PCVs) who first arrived in Guatemala in 1963. Since then, almost 5,200 have served in Guatemala, helping rural and urban families in cooperation with governmental and non-governmental organizations. Anna arrived with 134 other volunteers in health, youth, and food security programs. Anna was a youth development specialist.

Much has changed since I was a PCV in Guatemala in the 1970s. The world has become more complex and dangerous, leading to a greater focus on security issues within the Peace Corps, something I became aware of while interviewing for a Guatemala Country Director's position in 2014. About three-quarters of the way through the interview, I realized I had not been asked one question about program development or monitoring and evaluation - all the questions had related to potential security threats.

Later that evening, after my interview, I met the Program Director for Peace Corps Guatemala at a reception. He told me that the Peace Corps office had been moved from Guatemala City, the country capital, and the largest city in Central America, to a small rural site outside the town because it would be closer to the rural areas where the volunteers are based. However, others have since confirmed that it was due to security concerns.

I also learned that volunteers were not allowed to enter the capital due to concerns for their safety. Volunteers could no longer jump on "chicken buses" like I had used frequently as a volunteer but had to use Peace Corps-provided shuttles to and from their sites. The Peace Corps staff now included security personnel. When I contacted a volunteer about collaborating with a local Rotary International program in her area, she told me she would find it difficult to connect with them because she had to be home for a 6:00 p.m. curfew! Although informed that I qualified as a potential director, I decided not to pursue the opportunity.

What Do Guatemalans Think?
I turned to award-winning Guatemalan filmmaker and friend Luis Argueta for a Guatemalan perspective on the Peace Corps in his country. Luis, who received the Harris Wofford Global Citizenship Award from the National Peace Corps Association (NPCA), spoke to the attendees of the Peace Corps Connect to the Future: A Global Ideas Summit held in Austin, Texas, in July 2020. Some of his comments are included in the fall 2020 issue of *Worldview Magazine*, in an article titled "A Time to Reflect."

Luis and I have a particular interest in the emigration/immigration conundrum. He has paid close attention to forced displacement, forced migration, and asylum-seeking and asks a very timely question: "...even if borders today are closed, once they open...people will be forced again to leave their homes. What is the Peace Corps to do at a time like this? I think it is to go and work at the fundamental community level and help better conditions that are making it impossible for people to stay at home and be with their family and prosper and be healthy."

He goes on to say, "At the same time that we self-reflect on our role and our privileges, and the privileges of volunteers, we should look at the historical ties between the host countries and the U.S. ... the U.S. government is not issuing visas for my fellow Guatemalans to travel to the U.S., while there is a threat of cutting visas even for exchange students who pay full tuition at U.S. universities, let alone temporary workers who pick the crops in the fields of the U.S.. So, we must be conscious of these contradictions. And we must relearn the history between our countries."

He ends with that, although Peace Corps Volunteers reached home safely during the pandemic, "... this took them away from a place where they had committed to work - and where people without that privilege that choice had to remain in a more vulnerable position."

To that point, the school's director where Anna Zauner worked, says that her students are studying online, and some have reached out to Anna on their English assignments. But, some students have revealed that working from textbooks alone is complex, and some feel they aren't learning. These students don't know when their school will reopen, which is the case throughout Guatemala.

The Peace Corps in Guatemala
Peace Corps Director Jody Olsen was tasked with the unenviable job of evacuating 7,300 worldwide. It must have been painful, as the Peace Corps has been in her "blood for fifty-four years" (she volunteered in Tunisia in 1966). Her

comments on the future of the Peace Corps, made on July 18, 2020, began with, "We will be stronger for what we have been through together. The Peace Corps' mission of world peace and friendship is as relevant today as it was in 1961."

Peace Corps Guatemala Director of Programming and Training, Jeremy Boley, was still in Guatemala and gave me a heads-up on the Peace Corps' return status: "Peace Corps Guatemala is diligently elaborating the strategy to return volunteers to Guatemala. This includes close coordination with our partners at host country agencies, closely monitoring the pandemic's progress, and looking forward to welcoming volunteers into all four of our programs, including community economic development, agriculture, youth in development, and health."

He also confirmed that the security of volunteers is "of utmost importance and maintaining an Emergency Action Plan and having a system to monitor the location of volunteers are indispensable tools in ensuring the well-being of our volunteers."

Recent natural disasters that precipitated deadly landslides and flooding, which destroyed crops, impacted over 1.7 million Guatemalans. Government data shows acute malnutrition among under-fives rose by 80% last year compared to the previous year. Jeremy stated, "Since it takes time for communities to recover from the effects of these events, volunteers may find that their community development skills are needed in these areas. Agriculture volunteers, for example, may assist their work partners in training on soil conservation techniques that maximize infiltration during heavy rains and reduce flooding. Concerning migrant caravans (heading to the U.S.), volunteer efforts in our Youth in Development Program encourage youth to stay in school and develop job-related skills to improve their employment prospects in Guatemala. Our Community Economic Development volunteers will support income-generating activities that encourage development and growth within Guatemala. These efforts promote alternative pathways to migration."

A Time for Reflection

Although 134 volunteers were forced to evacuate, close to 5,200 Returned Peace Corps Volunteers (RPCVs), whose lives were impacted by their service in Guatemala, remain a positive influence on the country and the volunteers who will return. My experience as a volunteer indicates that no matter how effective I was, I learned more from Guatemalans than I was able to teach them, and what I learned would motivate me to continue supporting the most vulnerable populations in any way possible. One way to accomplish this is to fulfill the third objective of the Peace Corps, which is to promote a better understanding of other people on the part of Americans. The Peace Corps Writers Group lists 327 RPCV authors who have written two or more books and generated around 1,000 memoirs.

One such author, Mark Brazaitis, has written eight books, including ***Stories from Guatemala: The River of Lost Voices***, winner of the Iowa Short Fiction Award. He also wrote the script for the award-winning Peace Corps film ***How Far Are You Willing to Go to Make a Difference?***The best memoir among RPCVs/Guatemala would be Ellena Urbani's ***When I Was Elena.*** She has written for *The New York Times*, and her stories have been selected for inclusion in several collections and books about her Peace Corps service.

Much of my first book, ***Different Latitudes: My Life in the Peace Corps and Beyond***, occurred in Guatemala. I agree with Luis Argueta's observation about being conscious of the relationship between the U.S. and its host countries, and I included a chapter entitled "Guate mala Guate peor," which starts with a quote from writer Eduardo Galeano on ***Rigoberta: The Granddaughter of the Maya.***"This book relates to the dreams and nightmares of a land pulled apart from the army, raped by businessmen, lied to by politicians, despised by doctors." The CIA led a military intervention of Guatemala in 1954 with the overthrow of Arbenz and the elimination of essential changes like land reform, destroyed the opportunity to deal with the severe inequality and poverty facing most Guatemalans, especially in the highlands, and is the basis of many of the country's social ills today. These publications and the many presentations and materials written by other RPCVs help educate the public in the U.S. about the realities and needs of Guatemala and help inform U.S. policymakers. Also, RPCVs can do things that the Peace Corps can't as a government agency with certain norms placed on it by our country's foreign policy.

What Have We Learned?

The Peace Corps, like our country, has changed a good deal over the last sixty years. When President Kennedy asked, "Technicians or engineers, how many of you are willing to work in the Foreign Service and spend your lives traveling worldwide? … But your willingness to contribute part of your life to his country will depend on whether a free society can compete."

But as author and RPCV Paul Theroux points out, "It is impossible to imagine any politician—anyone at all—saying that today." And yet, the urge to serve, travel, and learn a new language will assure that some of the evacuated Peace Corps Volunteers will return, and many more will apply to volunteer in the "Land of the Eternal Spring."

This desire to serve and the actual economic downturn and impact of COVID-19 in the U.S. will accelerate the number of individuals willing to apply and serve in Guatemala. Based on my interview with the Peace Corps Program Director, Jeremy Boley, I think the organization is positioned to deal with some of the unique challenges facing them today, including the growing levels of hunger and malnutrition experienced by Guatemalans and issues like climate change.

Over the years, these 5,200 RPCVs have formed lifelong relationships and a series of organizations that continue to benefit Guatemala. Overall, 245,000 RPCVs have formed 180 affiliate groups, part of the National Peace Corps Association. These individuals and the alliances they've created with international groups take many forms and shapes. I'm a board member of Partnering for Peace, which promotes shared programs between Peace Corps Volunteers and Rotary International and has 1.2 million members worldwide and a strong presence in Guatemala. I'm also a member of Friends of Guatemala, which has provided scholarships benefiting children for over thirty years. More extensive chapters, like the affiliate in Washington D.C., have over 4,000 members and develop partnerships with non-governmental organizations.

No doubt, Returned Peace Corps Volunteers and some of the groups they've formed, along with the international community, will need to support local leaders' efforts to hold their government officials accountable by sending them to prison for corruption, as is the case with former president, Otto Perez Molina, and his vice president, Roxana Baldetti. And push for the return of U.N. agency CICIG (a powerful U.N.-backed commission formed to investigate corruption), which exposed over sixty corruption schemes, implicating officials in all three branches of the Guatemalan government. These alliances must support and attempt to protect the lives of local leaders and advocates fighting for fundamental rights, push for more influence in the government and the workplace, and support local rural alliances that promote economic development and education.

For the last fifty-seven years, the Peace Corps has been part of the development process in Guatemala. Now that the Peace Corps is preparing to send volunteers back to the field, they'll need to retool to meet such challenges as malnutrition, climate change, and a lack of primary health care.

Simultaneously, Returned Peace Corps Volunteers and their affiliate groups will need to continue telling the stories of Guatemalans and supporting the best programs and local leaders they can identify. Given the enthusiasm of the incoming volunteers and the commitment of the Returned Peace Corps Volunteers, in conjunction with local and international alliances promoting human rights and development, I have great expectations that the Peace Corps can help Guatemalans meet the new challenges of the future.

Chapter 13

HUGS NOT WALLS: BRINGING THE CHILDREN HOME

A sign hanging in the Anapra neighborhood of Juárez, Mexico, translates to "Hugs Not Walls." (Brittny Mejia / Los Angeles Times)

The separation of children from their families at the U.S. border in 2019 created one of the saddest and most contentious issues of an already complicated debate about immigration into the United States. The existing political frenzied discussions and false narratives it generates make it difficult, if not impossible, to turn this crisis into an opportunity to appreciate better the trauma caused by those children being separated from their families and the grassroots efforts to bring these families back together and deal with the negative impact of the experience.

Despite the trauma and pressures placed on immigrants, especially children, several individuals and groups around the country have stepped forward to support immigrant families and educate the public about their plight and why they deserve our respect and solidarity. These groups differ in religious beliefs, but share a commitment, compassion, an understanding and an appreciation of what immigrants mean to our communities.

Who can forget the video of the children behind a metal fence sitting on the floor with only a metallic blanket to keep them warm in the winter cold? Who can ignore the children's cries and sobs for "Mami" and the guard's pathetic response, taunting the children as being an orchestra of whiners, or the guards pulling small children out of one cell block and into another as they kick and scream, not knowing where their parents are or why these strangers are treating them so violently and with such disdain? Who can witness without empathy the agony of the mother whose son didn't recognize her after three months of separation and who wanted nothing to do with her, as he felt abandoned and betrayed?

According to a report issued by the Inspector General of the Department of Health and Human Services, the number of children separated from their families (2,700) was even more than initially stated. This number included 118 separated children taken between July and early November - after the administration halted the family separation effort because it had provoked a political firestorm and public outrage. According to the American Civil Liberties Union, the total number of children separated from their families since July 2017 is more than 5,400. Over 13,000 children are currently detained - the largest population ever - which has increased more than five-fold since last year.

Although previous administrations also separated minors from adults at the border in some instances - usually when they suspected the child had been smuggled in or the parent appeared unfit - the report documents a sharp increase in separations under President Trump. The actual number is still hazy due to the poor quality of the federal tracking system.

They Just Took Them?
Juana Francisca Bonilla de Canjura wiped tears from her face in the courtroom as she listened to the proceedings through a translation headset. In her hands, she clutched the passports of her two daughters: Ingrid, ten, and Fatima, twelve. They had come together from El Salvador and then were separated at the border. The bright blue documents were her only way of getting them back.

"I don't have any idea where they are," she'd told a Washington Post reporter shortly before the hearing began. "Nobody knows anything. Nobody says anything - lies. They said they were taking them for questioning, and we were only going to be apart for a moment. But they never came back. What pains me is the thought they are suffering without me," she said. As she spoke, a border patrol agent in green fatigues cut off the conversation.

In a McAllen, Texas courthouse, 71 disheveled immigrants caught illegally crossing the Rio Grande filled the courtroom, the defendants' shackles clanking as they sat on wooden benches. The federal magistrate started proceedings with, "Good morning. We're here to take up several criminal cases that allege that the defendants violated the immigration laws of the United States." According to a report by Michael Miller in the Washington Post, federal courtrooms in Texas, and across the Southwest, are being flooded with distraught mothers and fathers who have been charged with misdemeanor illegal entry and separated from their children, a practice decried by many as traumatizing and inhumane. Last month, a Honduran father separated from his wife and three-year-old son killed himself in a Texas jail cell.

Separation has more than psychological consequences, as no less than three Guatemalan children died when they were being processed through the overburdened government border control system, which often has inadequate medical staff. One Guatemalan girl, Jakelin Caal Maquin, who went into cardiac arrest from exposure during her grueling trip across the border, was taken to a local children's hospital, but it was too late. Nothing is worse for a parent than one of their children being born, then taken away, never to return, and hundreds more were separated and have yet to be located and reunited with their families.

Sister Mary McCauley, who witnessed the impact of the largest federal immigration raid on a business at a chicken and beef processing plant in Postville, Iowa, told me of a sixteen-year-old boy who told one of the volunteers, "I didn't come here to rob people or do bad things. I just came to work to earn money for my family. Why do people hate us so much?" An honest and timely question.

Although the administration seemed intent on making the overall experience as difficult as possible, they didn't have the necessary infrastructure to deal with the influx of children. In Phoenix, they began dropping busloads of families off at designated churches despite their inability to absorb all the new arrivals. The numbers were so great that ICE (Immigration and Customs Enforcement) agents began dropping them off at bus stations without support, as church groups and local charities scrambled to respond to the large influx of unannounced immigrants.

In a New York Times report, the number of detained migrant children has risen sharply since last summer. Over 1,600 migrant children have been sent, with little notice, on late-night voyages to a barren tent city in West Texas, where they do not receive schooling and have limited access to legal representation. These midnight voyages are playing out across the country as the federal government struggles to find room for record numbers of detained immigrant children.

Advocates of the "Hugs" or "Abrazos"
According to a "Fast Company" article by Gwen Moran, Julie Schwietert Collazo was listening to a radio interview in downtown Manhattan. The discussion featured Yeni Gonzalez Garcia, a Guatemalan mother seeking U.S. asylum detained in an Arizona immigrant detention center. Her daughter had been taken and placed in foster care in New York. According to her attorney, if she could post bail, she could relocate to New York and work to reunify with her daughter. So, the only thing separating her from her daughter was money, in this case, a $7,000 bond.

Julie thought, "Okay, that can't be that difficult." Julie and her husband had several friends concerned about the plight of families being separated at the border, so they set up a "Go Fund Me" page, which would be the catalyst for their new organization, Immigrant Families Together. They soon learned that Yeni could not be authorized to work until her application had been processed, so this would be a long-term commitment.

This didn't deter Julie, whose "Go Fund Me" effort raised $1 million, reuniting sixty families and supporting roughly one hundred families going through the asylum process, helping with everything from legal counsel to locating a place for them to live. Julie's success motivated others to raise funds to support asylum seekers, like a couple in Menlo Park, California. Already donors to the Refugee Immigrant Center for Education and Legal Services, a San Antonio, Texas, nonprofit focused on providing free and low-cost legal services, this couple decided to launch a Facebook fundraiser for the organization. It generated $20 million, tripling the group's annual budget and making it the largest fundraiser in Facebook history.

Others have responded to the immigration issue differently, from fundraising and financial support. Guatemalan American filmmaker Luis Argueta has been telling immigrants' stories for over ten years to overcome the misperceptions and fears about the "invasion" of caravans from the Northern Triangle of Central America. His films have been instrumental in educating Americans, bringing people together with better understanding and compassion, and providing concrete steps for his audiences to help newly arrived immigrants.

Although initially trained as an engineer, in the 1990s, Argueta began to focus on filmmaking. "I went back to my roots and told the story of the people of Guatemala both in fiction and documentary films, providing a better understanding of Guatemalans on a global platform." Argueta's career took a turn when he learned of the most extensive and most costly immigration raid carried out in the history of the U.S. Nine hundred heavily armed Federal Agents, supported by helicopters, state troopers, and prison buses, converged on Agriprocessors, Inc., in Postville, Iowa, which was the largest kosher meat packing plant in the United States at that time. Of the 389 arrested, three out of four (293) were Guatemalans.

"What I thought would be a four-day fact-finding trip has turned into eight years," Argueta told radio program KGOU's *World Views* in 2016. But in fact, this was when Argueta galvanized around the issue of immigration.

What impressed Argueta most about the Postville raid was the community's response, first in Postville and then in other neighborhoods around this little town in northwestern Iowa. People gathered to support the immigrants who had been left behind after the raid, and to support the relatives of those immigrants who were in jail. It was remarkable. Argueta says, "This impressed me so much that I said, "The story needs to be told, and it's not going to happen in four days," so I stayed two weeks and returned many more times. Twenty-nine. I began learning about the push factors that make people come to this country and decided I'd better go to Guatemala to see the communities from where they came."

So far, his experience in Postville has resulted in three documentaries about immigrants in Iowa and Minnesota and the small farm towns they call home.

"Something that struck me very much was how such a small Midwestern town could be such a microcosm of diversity," Argueta said. He saw immigrants from all over the world, including Guatemala, Mexico, Somalia, Ukraine, and Russia, who call Postville home. Argueta later traveled to his native Guatemala to visit the communities where these migrants originated. He wanted to learn why people chose to leave their homeland, which gave him the ideal perspective of both ends of this epic journey.

A chance encounter inspired Argueta's second film, *ABRAZOS* (2014), which tells the story of Abuelos y Nietos Juntos, a family reunification program. The film follows the journey of fourteen U.S. citizen children from Worthington, Minnesota, who travel to Ixchíguan, in the Department of San Marcos, Guatemala, to meet their relatives, grandparents, and even siblings for the first time.

Even though the number of children is small, they are a microcosm of the almost five million U.S. citizen children who live in mixed-status families. Argueta reflected, "I think that we really must think about those children who are part of the future of this country when we think about immigrants because they live in constant fear that their parents might be deported. And I don't think any child should live with that fear." Argueta says, "The film reflects the hopes, dreams, and fears of these transnational families who, after being separated for nearly two decades, can embrace each other, share stories, strengthen traditions, and begin to reconstruct their cultural identity."

He told one group he was raising funds to make the project possible. "I am convinced that after watching *ABRAZOS*, you will find resonances with your own life and family history no matter where you come from. I also hope that you will consider getting involved in some way. Your support will be crucial to develop and carry out an outreach campaign in partnership with key organizations working in areas of child development, children's rights, and mental health. I hope you agree - their stories need to be told."

Although the group did not sponsor any exchange trips after 2014, they discovered a need for transportation to the Immigration Court at Ft. Snelling, Minnesota, for those involved in the immigration process. This need was exceptionally high with the influx of children and youth seeking asylum across the border from 2014 to 2015. Not only can't they drive, but the family members they stay with don't generally have valid Minnesota driver's licenses. Hence, they need transportation to their court appearances, which are a three-hour drive away. Consequently, the group set up a system of volunteer drivers to help with this need, and along with several other Twin City organizations, they offered $25 gas cards to help them with travel expenses and their court appearances. One of the staff members accompanied them to court, as well.

The last film of his trilogy, *The U-Turn* (2017), tells the story of immigrant women and children who broke their silence about the abuses committed against them at the Agriprocessors, Inc. plant. Thanks to the community's solidarity that accompanied them and to the U Visa program, their lives and those of the people who walked along with them were transformed. The U Visa was established by Congress for victims of some crimes (in this case, hiring illegal or under-aged workers) who helped law enforcement investigate criminal activity.

Argueta has become an expert on the complex issues of immigration in the U.S. He has shown films at multiple college campuses and led discussions after the viewing. He has participated in various panels on the subject and has been honored due to his expertise. He recently presented screenings of *The U-Turn* at the University of Arizona and again at Arizona State University. After each presentation, he takes questions from all participants.

Margherita Tortora, Director at the New Haven Latin and Iberian Film Festival at Yale, said of Luis's visit there, "He has worked tirelessly to educate people about the human rights abuses against his people through his documentaries. His work puts human faces and personal stories into the discussions about immigration in the United States. He is bringing down the wall! Thank you, Luis Argueta! I am looking forward to your presentation at the Yale Law School..."

Lessons Learned
Argueta shared more of his experience around immigration during a radio interview with host Suzette Grillot on KGOU's *World Views* program in 2016:

Argueta: *I also just came back from Guatemala from working on an advertising campaign for an agency in Washington that is aimed at stopping this phenomenon (caravans). This situation is not going to stop until we change the structural conditions of the sending communities. But this campaign is aimed to make people at least think twice about sending their kids. And so I have seen the phenomenon. It's mind-boggling. However, we really must understand that until we address, in a very strong fashion, what is pushing people away, as well as what is pulling them, we're going to continue to have these phenomena.*

Argueta: *People know the risks of sending their kids but, when the families live lives that are full of risks every day, when the risk of a child becoming a member of a gang, or maybe not reaching age fifteen because he or she is killed, they're ... sending them north - at least they have some hope. And they also see the results of others that have succeeded in this trip. It's a terrible situation, the issues that immigrants have to face on a daily basis, and that's something that I wish on nobody. And they don't do it lightly.*

Interviewer Suzette Grillot: *Issues like deportation and building of walls and, you know, increasing law enforcement on these issues. I mean, how are some of the people that you've been working with, how is this going to affect the work that you do, first of all, and do you have any projects planned, and what is the response and reaction to some of the immigrants that you're working with?*

Argueta: *Well, you know, one of the reasons I've been doing this for all these years is because I realize that often in the national conversation about immigration we get lost in the numbers. We talk about eleven million, quote unquote, illegals, and then we forget the human face of immigrants – and that is what my work aims to do, to bring out that human face, to make us realize that in every immigrant we do have another human being that is just like us. You* *know, "There, but for the grace of God, go I" means something that I have really come to feel very strongly. I had the privilege of going to meet Pope Francis two years ago and gave him a copy of my first two films and I said to him, "These are the stories of the immigrants that have touched my heart and changed my life." And that's what I hope to do with these films, and with this conversation, because I go to universities, faith-based communities, and conferences, and engage in one-to-one or small group conversations with the hope that we will be able to recognize ourselves in the immigrants. At the same time, I think it is extremely important that we understand the root causes of the situation. This is not something new. This is not something that only happens in the U.S. It's happening globally. So, we must all really roll up our sleeves.*

Argueta: *Also, on the other hand, realize that there are laws in this country that cannot change from one day to the next. There are things that the president can do with the stroke of a pen, but also there are a lot of other things that he alone cannot do and will need to change. You know, the support of Congress. So hopefully, our humanity will prevail, and our common sense will prevail. This country needs immigrants. We cannot say we're not going to stop. We're not going to stop people from sending remittances to Mexico, Guatemala, or El Salvador because those economies would collapse, and it will backfire.*

Argueta was presented the Harris Wofford Global Citizen Award at the June Peace Corps Connect Conference in Austin, Texas. The award is given to individuals who live in the country where they were influenced by a Peace Corps volunteer and where they promote the values of this organization. As part of the vetting process for the award, Argueta revealed that "My experience with the Peace Corps taught me one of the valuable lessons of my life: to treat others as one would wish to be treated - the Golden Rule."

Just before the awards ceremony, Argueta was screening *ABRAZOS* when the founder of Abuelos y Nietos Juntos walked in with four of the children who had made the visit to their grandparents seven years earlier. They were now young adults and expressed their plans to attend college and pursue various professions. Several of them had returned to visit their families in Guatemala after the initial visit, and all four were in the front row to witness the presentation of the Global Citizen award to Argueta. During his acceptance speech, Argueta challenged the participants with, "At times like the present, when powerful winds of isolation and intolerance are blowing, it is more important than ever to speak out - to find our commonality as human beings, roll up our sleeves and to work to nurture the hope for peace in the world."

More than a thousand children separated from their families have not been reunited, nor do their parents know where they are. Despite all the rhetoric about building walls, the number of undocumented migrants entering the country has reached a ten-year high. Eleven million undocumented immigrants are in limbo, some for over twenty years, and no integrated immigration reform is on the horizon.

And yet, the number of groups, the advocates like Julie and Luis, whose films are receiving more attention, not to mention the thousands who have given small gifts to cover legal fees, no matter what the final solution, will continue to put the needs of the migrant children and their families' well-being before the political bickering, hate talk, and misinformation. All of these actions are a reason for hope.

Chapter 14

JUSTICE & RESPONSIBILITY: THE PLIGHT OF THE IMMIGRANTS FROM CENTRAL AMERICA

"NO ONE LEAVES HOME UNLESS HOME IS THE MOUTH OF A SHARK." WARSAN SHIRE FROM LUTHERAN IMMIGRATION AND REFUGEE SERVICES

Migrant caravans, made up of large groups of children and adults from the Northern Triangle of Central America, heading to our border to seek safety and a better life is problematic for those coming and those waiting to arrive in the U.S. According to the Customs and Border Patrol, the

influx of undocumented immigrants has reached a ten-year high, with 66,450 entering recently.

The frenzied political debate and the false narratives in 2019 made it difficult, if not impossible, to turn this crisis into an opportunity to appreciate why so many continue to seek refuge here and to understand our role and that of our government in sorting out the situation, responding in a humanitarian way to those coming, and creating some viable solutions to our immigration policies in the future.

Although smaller caravans have headed toward our borders in the past, the growing influx of immigrants raised further challenges and complexities around the existing crisis. With eleven million undocumented workers in the country who contribute to society but reap none of the benefits of full membership, it creates exploitation and a threat to our democracy.

There are five factors worth scrutinizing to understand the situation better: who they are and what they want, what pushes people away from their homes, what pulls them towards the U.S., what impact our government's policies and those of their home country governments have on the process, and some of the lessons learned in dealing with the situation positively.

So, Who Are They?

The ongoing cable television coverage of the most recent "Caravan" has provided a window into the world of these people, most coming from Honduras, but some from Guatemala and El Salvador - including entire families and many young children making this arduous journey into the unknown. These are not the highly trained hi-tech experts corporate Silicon Valley executives seek. Guatemalan filmmaker Luis Argueta has spent the last ten years telling the stories of immigrants and recently completed the third of his documentary series. He's become an expert on the complex issues of immigration into the U.S. and has shown films at multiple college campuses and led discussions after the viewing. He has participated in various panels on the subject and has been honored due to his expertise. He recently presented, and made presentations, at the University of Arizona in Tucson and Arizona State University in Tempe. Argueta tells the story of a group of immigrant women and children who broke their silence about the abuses committed against them at the Agriprocessors, Inc. in Postville, Iowa, and thanks to the solidarity of the community that accompanied them and the U Visa, their lives and the lives of those that walked along with them were transformed.

The sense of desperation of many crossing the border is best summed up in the last paragraph of Francisco Cantu's *The Line Becomes a River*, from an immigrant whose attempt to cross the border failed after he witnessed several of his group, including a small girl, left behind in the desert to die:

[]*If they know the reality, the judges in the United States know they are sending people to their deaths. They are sending people to commit suicide. I will do anything to be on the other side. To be honest, I would rather be in a []prison in the U.S. and see my boys once a week through the glass than to stay here and be separated from my family. At least I would be closer to them. So, you see, there is nothing that can keep me from crossing. My boys are not dogs to be abandoned in the street. I will walk through the desert for five days, eight days, ten days, whatever it takes to be with them. I'll eat []grass, I'll eat bushes, I'll eat cactus, I'll drink filthy cattle water, I'll drink nothing at all. I'll run and hide from "la migra." I'll pay the mafias whatever I have to. They can take my money, they can rob my family, they can lock me away, but I will keep coming back. I will keep crossing again and again until I make it, until I am together again with my family. "No, no me quedo aqui. Voy a seguir intentando pasar."*

The Push Factor

When I first arrived in an isolated area of the highlands of Guatemala in 1971 as a Peace Corps Volunteer, I realized that something was seriously wrong when I noticed many small graves in a cemetery outside the village of Calapté. The graves were so tiny that I assumed that the villagers buried their dogs there. Then, one weekend when the villagers were drinking and carrying on for some unknown reason, I asked the head teacher, Don Hector, what was being celebrated.

He explained that the villagers were celebrating the deaths of the *Angelitos*, babies who had died before their first birthday. He said that this was a happy time since they went directly to heaven because they hadn't committed any sins. Happy time? Not in my book. Years later, Frank La Rue, a longtime human rights activist in Guatemala and former United National official, told *The New York Times* in 2010, "You can only explain that (50,000 unaccompanied children fleeing north to the U.S. in 2014) when you have a state that doesn't work."

The state does work, but for very few, like the 2% of the population who owned 84% of the land after the armed conflict in 1995. Most Guatemalans, especially the Maya population, have small, unproductive plots of land that force them to the south coast to harvest cash crops such as coffee or look for a job in the capital city. This exploitation goes back to Spanish Colonial rule when some Maya communities were forced to supply a *reparto*, which involved a third of their male residents laboring on Spanish-owned plantations in nine-month shifts. Future Guatemalan regimes promoted this form of forced labor through the 19th century. This situation has been exacerbated over the years due to an incredible population increase from three million Guatemalans in 1950 to an estimated seventeen million today.

Eventually, these egregious inequities, combined with the population explosion, resulted in a period of violence lasting from 1960 to the "Peace Accord" in 1996, which cost the lives of over 200,000 people, mainly from the Maya population in the *highlands*. In 1995, when I led a donor tour to the Province of Quiché with *Food for the Hungry*, I came across pictures drawn by the children depicting planes dropping bombs (and sometimes napalm) on their homes.

The Quiché province would suffer more assassinations and murders than others in Latin America. In *The Art of Political Murder: Who Killed the Bishop?*Guatemalan/American author Francisco Goldman presents some of the testimony from the "REMHI" report by the Catholic Church on government/army abuses in places like Santa Maria Tzejá, Quiché: *The señora was pregnant. With a knife, they cut open her belly to pull out her little baby boy. And they killed them both. And the muchachitas (little girls) playing in the trees near the house they cut off their little heads with machetes.*

Those who were able to escape often wandered for years in the forests before they felt safe enough to return to their homes. Although the army and their para-military groups were responsible for most of the recorded massacres, some were attributed to the local guerrilla groups, and in 1995 a truce was made—a "peace" was declared. Of course, the children wouldn't be the only target of this state-run violence; often those who reported it, like Bishop Juan Gerardi, would be assassinated by military thugs long after the "peace accord" had been signed.

I recently interviewed two Guatemalan immigrants while volunteering at a shelter in a local church in downtown Phoenix. Hector and Felix brought their wives and children from the Guatemala highlands. Both were small farmers forced to leave due to a protracted drought in which the annual dry season, or *canicula*, lasted much longer than usual, killing most of their crops, their primary food source. Despite the risks, they believed it was worth it compared to their seemingly hopeless situation back home in Guatemala.

In one of three recent articles on Guatemalan immigrants in *The New Yorker*, the author confirmed that over 65% of children suffer from malnutrition, one of the highest rates in the Western Hemisphere. Hector and Felix's communities are part of the expanding swath of Central America known as the "dry corridor." It begins in Panama and snakes northwest through Costa Rica, Nicaragua, El Salvador, Honduras, Guatemala, and parts of southern Mexico. One Guatemalan climate scientist at the Universidad del Valle said, "Extreme poverty may be the primary reason people leave... but climate change is intensifying all the existing factors." This phenomenon is underscored in a series of articles in the Guatemalan daily, *La Prensa Libre*, which reports that farmers don't know when to plant crops to avoid these dry periods, with possible total loss of their harvests.

At the Phoenix shelter, Felix also mentioned he had no other option but to leave his home, as he'd opted to mortgage the land where the family grew its food. "I'll pay it off with the money I earn here."

The Pull Factor

The magnet bringing families to the north would include something they lack at home: a "living wage." The money, or "remittances" sent by those who have successfully crossed the border, are the first or second key income generator of most Central American countries, right up there with tourism. According to the International Organization for Immigration, remittances to Guatemala have exceeded $8.5 billion. Some U.S.-based businesses take advantage of their workers' illegal status, as was recently revealed by Univision TV, which reported on two illegal workers at one of President Donald Trump's golf courses in New Jersey. After a *New York Times* report, two Trump properties, which included the Trump National Golf Club, fired two dozen undocumented workers. About eight million undocumented workers are part of the U.S. labor force, and it's an open secret that they use fake documents to get hired.

The Impact of Government Policies

U.S. economic and foreign policies impact our ability to deal with this immigration crisis. So far, the Trump administration has referred to immigrants as freeloaders, criminals, and terrorists or, conversely, consistently poor and vulnerable, which has led to an inaccurate narrative at best. Separating children from their parents without a plan to reunite them as part of a "deterrent" was a miscalculation, with no appreciation or respect for the families involved, not to mention the considerable trauma caused. Stirring up fear to justify the construction of an enormous wall is also less than productive. Most recently, the U.S. Border Patrol and ICE have been dropping large groups of families at local churches in Phoenix because they cannot absorb all of them. The churches are left to care for and eventually place them with family members until their trial for asylum, which can take up to a year.

The hate, misunderstandings, and trauma caused by these policies pale compared to the unstated strategy of using the Arizona desert to channel illegal immigrants to their demise. Francisco Cantu, the author of *The Line Becomes a River*, shared the Arizona Death Map, which uses dots to represent 3,244 migrant deaths in the desert between Nogales and Yuma between 1999 and 2018. Some of the dots represent multiple deaths. Humane Borders accumulated the data to help visualize the number of people whose deaths go unknown or unappreciated. Since the most effective border control tends to focus close to border towns, this large stretch of desert covers so much space that someone must walk up to one hundred miles through the desolation and brutal heat before finding a road that can take them anywhere without being detected—a sad example of how violence is normalized in our society.

Unfortunately, U.S. foreign policy has been instrumental in creating many conditions that push those from some of the most isolated parts of their home country to the north. The U.S. has consistently intervened throughout Latin America and has supported the most repressive regimes. In the early 1950s, the U.S.-based fruit company United Fruit, or "La Frutera," exacerbated the poor land distribution in Guatemala, as the company owned over half a million acres of the country's richest land, but left eighty-five percent of it uncultivated. La Frutera employed almost fifty thousand workers in Central America (most were Central Americans, except for management by U.S. citizens), including fifteen thousand on just two of its many plantations in Guatemala. It owned the only railroad and controlled the critical port of Puerto Barrios.

United Fruit's interests were the same as those of the U.S. (what's suitable for the Frutera is good for the U.S.). U.S. Secretary of State John Foster Dulles and his brother, Director of the CIA, Allen Dulles, were both partners in the United Fruit law firm, Sullivan & Cromwell. These two powerful siblings' "secret" history was brilliantly divulged in Stephen Kinzer's *The Brothers*.

In 1950, Jacobo Arbenz was elected President of Guatemala and began promoting social reform policies and land reform, which was a problem for the country's largest landowner, United Fruit, which carried out a propaganda campaign that turned the U.S. government against the new regime. American newspaper headlines included such inflammatory leads as "Red Front Tightens Grip on Guatemala." This led to a coup d'état in 1954. A new president, Carlos Castillo Armas, took dictatorial powers, banning all political parties, torturing and imprisoning political opponents, and reversing the social reforms of the Guatemala revolution; in effect, they dealt a death blow to Guatemalan democracy and reinforced the structural land tenure system that was keeping the majority of Guatemalans on the margin of the larger economy.

The U.S.'s inability and lack of political will to control the proliferation of drugs within its borders has also impacted the region by allowing the drug cartels to gain ever-growing financial and political influence. Some 70% of the U.S. cocaine supply has been channeled through Honduras, resulting in one of the highest murder rates in the world. According to David Grann's article in *The New Yorker* magazine, "A

Murder Foretold":

[]Overwhelmed by drug gangs, grinding poverty, social injustice, and an []abundance of guns, it's no wonder that violent crime rates have been sky-high. In 2009, fewer civilians were reported killed in the war zone of Iraq than were shot, stabbed, or beaten to death in Guatemala," and a staggering majority of homicides - 97% - go unsolved. Grann stated, "The []incredible power and influence of the drug cartels is now being revealed by the trial of the "Chapo," demonstrating how his bribes went to the highest level of Mexican government officials."

A recent proliferation of *maras*, or gangs, began with the mass deportation of Los Angeles criminals to Central America, particularly El Salvador, in the mid-1990s. The MS-13, for example, became an international gang that spread through the continental U.S. and Central America. Most members are Salvadorans, and its history is closely tied to the U.S.–El Salvador relationship, especially regarding U.S. interventions in the Salvadoran Civil War in the 1980s. In 2011, the United Nations Office on Drugs and Crime reported that El Salvador had the highest number of gang members in Central America, with *thirty-two thousand*.

So, one can see how centuries of political abuse, violence, and a depleted infrastructure—schoolhouses with no books and hospitals and clinics with no medication and often a lack of doctors, have created despair, which is why families continue to leave their homes looking for a haven and an opportunity to educate their children. And why so many are seeking asylum instead of simply looking for work.

So, what are the Northern Triangle Central American administrations doing to stem the flow of immigrants? Let us look at Guatemala. To begin with, although the United States encouraged civilian rule and elections in Guatemala in 1985, the subsequent elections were deficient in substantive democratic reforms. Historian Suzanne Jones wrote: For the most part, from 1986 through 1995, civilian presidents allowed the army to rule from behind the scenes. After an initial decline, death squad violence and other abuses by the military increased significantly in the late 1980s. Excessive influence from the military, human rights abuses, and corruption have hampered subsequent regimes.

One program that both the U.S. and Central American governmental agencies are developing is the Alliance for Prosperity Northern Triangle. The program promotes local economic, health, and infrastructural support to the poorest provinces, which export the most refugees. According to the local newspaper, *Prensa Libre*, some $27 million from the U.S. will be focused on the most vulnerable towns and provinces. The program reflects a realization that, under existing conditions, the outflow of rural Indigenous groups will continue. Although it's a step in the right direction, the impact of this initiative will be limited by corruption, as Guatemala has one of the highest rates of pilferage in the world.

[]I experienced this first-hand in 2001. After a TV appearance with the MAP International (Medical Assistance Programs) CEO on local TV with Guatemala's First Lady, Evelyn Morataya, our cab driver told us he had seen us on TV with *"la primera dama de la corrupcion"* (the first Lady of Corruption). So even the humblest Guatemalan knew what was going on. Her husband, President Alfonso Portillo, would eventually be extradited to the U.S. and charged with laundering $70 million in Guatemalan funds through U.S. bank accounts.

More recently, the president, Otto Perez Molina, and former vice president, Roxana Baldetti, were imprisoned for corruption, thanks to the efforts of the UN anticorruption commission, CICIG (International Commission Against Impunity in Guatemala). Although the campaign slogan of the existing president, Jimmy Morales, was "Neither Corrupt Nor A Thief," in January of 2017, his older brother, a close adviser, and the adviser's son were arrested on corruption and money laundering charges. Eight months later, Morales ordered the expulsion of Colombian Ivan Velasquez, Commissioner of the CICIG, after it not only began investigating claims that his party took illegal donations, including from drug traffickers, but also asked the Guatemalan Congress to strip him of immunity from prosecution, which the Congress would refuse to do, thus assuring that the impunity of Guatemala's ruling class would continue unchecked.

The Guatemalan Congress is considering a law that offers total amnesty to those involved in the abuses and massacres during the civil conflict, effectively eliminating any level of accountability. Other abuses include death threats and killings of elected officials, witnesses, members of the judiciary, and others involved in investigations of government corruption and human rights crimes, as well as violent evictions, labor rights violations, and other human rights violations in the context of agrarian disputes involving thousands of rural families, according to the Guatemalan Human Rights Commission.

Lessons Learned

At this point in our country's history, we can choose to be part of the problem or begin to work towards practical solutions to the immigration issues, challenging us, as well as Mexico and the countries in Central America. As U.S. citizens, we must appreciate that we are connected culturally, economically, and politically to the people in Central America. According to a recent NPR report, remittances from Guatemalans working in the U.S. are one of the most important income sources for the country.

Also, our country's foreign policy, which favored a small oligarchy supported by a strong military, has created much of the injustice described above. The U.S.'s inability to limit the use of illegal drugs has much to do with the poverty and violence currently pushing people out of Central America to the U.S. I agree with filmmaker Luis Argueta's comments at his Arizona State University (ASU) presentation that those who ignore this reality and support the existing government's policies are "complicit" in perpetuating the ongoing influx of undocumented family members.

Those escaping violence and abject poverty in Central America will continue to seek asylum and work in the United States, especially those with family ties here. No wall, no matter how big, tall, or wide, will stop the ongoing influx of immigrants.

Instead of creating fear about "invading" insurgents, we must learn about and appreciate who these people are and treat them more humanely when they arrive here, as well as support the development efforts in the sending provinces in Central America in order to encourage and enable young people to stay and raise their families in their home countries.

Chapter 15

CROSSING BORDERS, BUILDING BRIDGES

Maria Martin(far right) and Luis Argueta at the Peace Corps Connect Conference

I first learned about Maria Martin at the Peace Corps Connect Conference in Austin, Texas, in 2019. I witnessed Guatemalan filmmaker, Luis Argueta, whom I had helped nominate, receive the Wofford Harris Global Citizenship Award. During the conference, Argueta participated in a discussion panel titled "Beyond Borders" with Maria Martin, the director of *The Gracias Vida Center for Media*, and several immigration experts. I noticed that both Maria and Luis mentioned that one of their primary goals was to "change the narrative" around Guatemalan migrants and give them a "human" face so they would be treated with the dignity and respect they deserve. The conversation then examined the historic exodus from Central America and the humanitarian crisis at the U.S. southern border. Some panelists underscored the need for policy solutions and opportunities for the Peace Corps community to act.

Two years passed before I heard of Maria again, this time on a program about emigration from Guatemala that aired on the public radio program *Reveal*. The program focused on Todos Santos, Huehuetenango and dealt with the challenges that forced local villagers to flee their homes and go north to the U.S. to make a living. In researching, I discovered that Maria was the founder of the Gracias Vida Media Center, based in Antigua, and then I learned about her new book, ***Crossing Borders, Building Bridges: A Journalist's Heart in Latin America.***

This book is an inspiring account of the author's decades of work as a Latina radio journalist across cultures, languages, and borders. She shares a series of fascinating stories and photographs in the book to describe her life's journey. Maria was introduced to bilingual radio in northern California in the mid-70s and went on to volunteer for the Somos Chicanas program, where she was allowed to interview Cesar Chavez, the iconic leader of the farm worker movement.

Eventually, Maria became the senior producer of *Latino USA*, where she reported on immigration from a policy and a human interest story perspective. One of her assignments with *Latino USA* included an investigation into the disappearance of Sister Dianna Ortiz, who was abducted and tortured in Guatemala in 1989. This led to the investigative report, *The Betrayal of Sister Dianna Ortiz and Surviving Torture: The Search for Healing.*

For decades, the Guatemalan government had been known for its human rights abuses, but this story had an added layer because of the nun's assertion that an American, "Alejandro," was present in the torture chamber. The author's ongoing research discredited the official explanation that the nun was a victim of mistaken identity (with a guerrilla leader), which was not plausible since, according to the author, Sister Dianna lacked the Spanish fluency of a native speaker.

The report's broadcast date was scheduled for the tenth anniversary of Ortiz's abduction and would be the author's most ambitious documentary to date. She considered it a labor of love. In the end, Maria gained Sister Dianna's trust and was grateful to Sister Dianna for allowing her to share her story. Sister Dianna became an outspoken human rights activist and advocate for torture victims; Martin received the Robert F. Kennedy Journalism Award for her work.

Maria Martin would go on to train rural and provincial journalists throughout Latin America, but especially in Guatemala. She counteracted the tendency for big-city journalists to look down on local reporters when they came to the provinces. Eventually, she would establish the Gracias Vida Media Center in Antigua.

Her commitment and vision for the future are reflected in her presentation in 2015 at a University of Texas event commemorating four decades of work in public radio: "Lives and careers come in cycles... Maybe now it's your turn to give back to that mentor - that person who gave you support..." Her admonishment was to "pay it forward, pay it back."

Mandalit del Barco, Arts and Culture Correspondent for National Public Radio, said it best: "The wonderful Maria Martin has inspired generations to follow her lead. So many of us working in public radio today can testify how influential she's been."

After witnessing her contributions to the panel at the Peace Corps Connect Conference and then reading her book, it became clear that Maria would be a natural addition to the documentary on emigration we began working on two years ago, ***Guatemala: Trouble in the Highlands***, after an article I wrote with the same title was highlighted in the July 2019 issue of *Revue Magazine*. In the article, I reported that climate change, unemployment, and relentless grinding poverty underpin the current migration crisis. The historical reality of the land, economic inequality, and the nationwide infestation of the narcotics trade led to nearly total government dysfunction.

This narrative would morph into the production of a documentary film, which was highlighted in the February 2020 issue of *Revue Magazine*. At that time, we reported that our focus would be what has happened in the past, what is currently occurring to fuel the U.S. border crisis, and lastly, what can be done to change the course of a cruel history. Our production team (which includes award-winning cinematographer Hal Rifken) had planned to have the project done by the end of 2020. Then, all international travel was canceled due to the COVID-19 pandemic. On the positive side, this delay allowed us to research our story further, including learning how other documentaries had dealt with the issues of interest to us.

Then, we were introduced to the work of Pamela Yates and the Skylight group, who focus on amplifying the voice of constituencies battling for social justice. Their most impressive documentary, *500 Years: Life in Resistance*, was filmed in 2017. This documentary follows the trial of former Guatemalan President Efrain Rios Montt for genocide against the country's Indigenous Maya population in the 1980s and the popular uprising that ensued after the trial, ultimately leading to the toppling of then President Otto Perez Molina. It is the third film in a trilogy, including *When the Mountains Tremble* and *Granito: How to Nail a Dictator*. Skylight is presently working on a new feature-length documentary, *Borderland*.

Having reviewed all these impressive productions, we realized they had already told the story of the Guatemalan Civil War and the U.S. involvement and eventual intervention. Additionally, many compelling stories had already been told by Guatemalan families who had been forced to flee their homes and head north, so what could we focus on which others hadn't?

Fortunately, Maria Martin reminded us of the paltry number of Maya representatives in the Guatemalan Congress (10% of the approximately 160) and that the number of Maya leaders killed or disappeared was growing by the day. She then suggested we tell our story from the Maya leadership perspective and focus on the growth of the Maya political movement, which resonated with the entire documentary team.

With that, we recruited Maria to be our executive producer. After all, we concluded, she had already researched the issues we were focusing on and had a wealth of experience training Maya radio journalists who could help us develop this new storyline on the root causes of why 50% of the country's population has yet to be adequately represented in the governmental structure of Guatemala.

This revised version of *Trouble in the Highlands* explores the tumultuous history of Guatemala's Indigenous communities and why the Maya remain desperately poor, exploited, and outside the corridors of political power, how the lack of Indigenous representation in government affects all aspects of life - the quality of schools, the availability of health care in rural areas, and respect for Indigenous culture and traditions. Through the eyes of Maya academics, activists, and political leaders, the documentary explores why so many are leaving and what is being done to reverse the economic and social stagnation that causes it.

We have also introduced a new segment showing how Bolivia's Indigenous leaders achieved political success over twenty years. There is no questioning the success of Evo Morales' political party, MAS, which elected the first Indigenous president in Bolivian history, and scores of Indigenous representatives. But Bolivia also offers a cautionary tale for Guatemala's political activists. Morales suffered many political setbacks during his years in power, but despite his failures, the standard of living for many of Bolivia's Indigenous communities rose dramatically.

Working with us to develop ***Trouble in the Highlands*** will fulfill Maria Martin's goal at the end of her book, ***Crossing Borders, Building Bridges***. "I will continue contributing through public and independent media in the U.S. and Latin America. I will tell stories - in English and Spanish - that touch people's minds and hearts, writing narratives that strive to improve cultural understanding among people."

Chapter 16

TROUBLE IN THE HIGHLANDS: A DOCUMENTARY FILM PRODUCTION

Maya women and a child

As I have previously stated, climate change, unemployment, and relentless grinding poverty are the underpinnings of the current migration crisis. There is also the historical reality of land and economic inequality and the nationwide infestation of the narcotics trade, leading to near-total government dysfunction.

Guatemala: Trouble In the Highlands, which began production several months ago, will spotlight what has happened in the past, what is currently occurring to fuel the U.S. border crisis, and what can be done to change the course of a cruel history. The production team expected to have the film done at the end of this year.

Through the eyes of three generations, the Estrada family tells the stories of how migration has traumatized their

Guatemalan village of Cajolá. Following family members, grandfather Aapo, son Eduardo, and granddaughter Izabella, ***Guatemala: Trouble In the Highlands*** will give viewers an up-close and personal understanding of this crisis.

According to the U.S. Customs and Border Patrol, in 2018, the influx of undocumented immigrants into the United States reached a ten-year high of more than 115,000, surpassing that in early 2019. The Pew Research Center reports that Guatemalans represent the second largest group of undocumented Latino immigrants (after El Salvador) trying to enter the U.S. The world watched as streams of people walked, rode, and took perilous train rides across hundreds of miles to reach the U.S. border. Where once the majority of these migrants were young males seeking work, the latest influx includes families and children, many of whom seek asylum.

The sharp political divide in the U.S. along partisan lines has made dialogue ineffective and a documentary film production like***Guatemala: Trouble in the Highlands***nearly impossible. Public opinion is equally divided, either sympathetic toward those seeking asylum or demonizing the migrants as thieves, drug dealers, and rapists.

The migrants' reasons for fleeing Guatemala are as diverse as the geography of the Guatemalan Highlands. Those planning to leave know it is dangerous to make the trip, but they are desperate. Initial interviews have been recorded in the U.S. and Guatemala, and additional interviews are lined up.

The script is in the draft stage, and planning is underway for the next production trip to Guatemala. As the producer, I have an MA in Latin American Studies from the University of Texas in Austin; I spent over forty years with groups helping in developing countries. My book, ***Different Latitudes: My Life in the Peace Corps and Beyond***, was recognized by the Arizona Literary Association literary contest for non-fiction. Over twenty of my articles have been published in literary magazines, and one essay, "Hugs not Walls: Returning the Children," won the Arizona Authors Association 2019 Literary Contest.

The director/cinematographer, Hal Rifken, has worked for numerous cable and broadcast networks domestically and abroad. His Peace Corps experience in Bolivia has led him to projects that explore intercultural issues, particularly as they relate to Latin America. The editor met him as a board member of Partnering for Peace, which tries to strengthen the partnership between Rotarians and Returned Peace Corps Volunteers. Rifken would subsequently travel to Costa Rica, the Dominican Republic, and South Africa, producing promotional videos for that partnership.

He completed a documentary on the Shanghai Quartet. This five-year project followed the string quartet to concerts and festivals around the United States, Asia, Europe, and Latin America (*Behind the Strings premiered on PBS in October 2023*).

Editor Tracy Cring is an award-winning editor with over thirty feature films to her credit. The films she's worked on have been widely distributed, won multiple awards, and been appreciated by audiences across the globe. NBC Nightly News featured her work for Danseur. Recently, *No History of Violence*, which she edited throughout production for four years, was honored for its social and humanitarian efforts.

The critical consultant Alana De Joseph's latest feature is a documentary production of the institutional history of the Peace Corps; Alana was associate producer of the PBS documentaries *The Greatest Good* (about the U.S. Forest Service) and *Green Fire* (about conservationist Aldo Leopold), with screenings at twenty-nine film festivals from Colorado to India and New Zealand. She sat down with the editor and his wife in Denver to discuss strategies to access funding from foundations and film associations and became an essential asset to the effort.

Documentary Postscript:

Despite four years of hard work with fellow returned Peace Corps volunteer and cinematographer Hal Rifken, and unique collaboration on many levels from so many people, we decided to shut down the production of our documentary, ***Trouble in the Highlands***. We did come close in 2020, as we had a foundation's commitment to underwrite a production trip Hal was to begin. Three days before the trip, the airport and borders into Guatemala were summarily shut down due to COVID-19. The pandemic put the documentary on hold for over two years. In the process, we lost our underwriting. . . and our momentum.

The production process has been a revealing journey. I've learned much and made many friends along the way. I wrote my first article on the theme for the summer issue of *WorldView Magazine* in 2019 and then republished it in *Revue Magazine*. Over the next few years, they published eight of my articles on immigration/ Guatemala. Hal Rifken, our director and cinematographer, made one production trip to Cajola, Guatemala, with the help of activists Caryn Maxim and Eduardo Jimenez, from which we edited two trailers, the most recent of which can be found on my website under "Documentary."

After getting to know Guatemalan anthropologist Victor Montejo and filmmaker Luis Argueta, it became increasingly clear that we needed to refocus our narrative from the perspective of Guatemalans, so we began interacting with them.

New productions team members included Executive Producer Maria Martin, an award-winning Latina journalist who reports from Antigua, Guatemala, for NPR's *Latino USA*, among other media outlets. Consultants Demetrio Cojti and his daughter, Avex Cojti, are academics from Guatemala's Kaqchikel region. Professor Cojti has a Ph.D. in Social Communications from Leuven, Belgium, and Avex Cojti works for Cultural Survival, an organization aiming to foster a future that respects and honors Indigenous Peoples' inherent rights. I enjoyed my Zoom interviews with Avex and her father about the challenges and nuances in the Maya community—seen by two generations of Maya activists.

Based on Hal's experience in Bolivia as a Peace Corps volunteer, we recruited several Bolivian leaders to open a dialogue with Maya leaders to explore the different experiences between the Indigenous populations. Both countries have large Indigenous communities. The Mayas only sent six members to Congress out of one hundred and four during the twelve years Evo Morales was the president of Bolivia. During this time, the Constitution was translated into Indigenous languages and played a vital role in the government.

This idea seemed more plausible after reading an article in NACLA, "Could Thelma Cabrera Become the Next Evo Morales?"This report states, "In Guatemala's last presidential elections, in 2019, Thelma Cabrera shocked the Guatemalan political establishment. As the candidate for the *Movimiento para la Liberación de Los Pueblos party* (MLP), a savvy social media campaign helped her earn an unexpected 10% of the vote. She finished fourth and missed the runoff, but placed herself at the forefront of Indigenous politics in the country. It was the most successful presidential run by an Indigenous person in Guatemala's modern history – the only other was by Nobel Prizewinner Rigoberta Menchú in 2007, who won 3% of the vote.

What were the underlying reasons for the contrast, and what might Guatemalan leaders take away from such a dialogue? We'd call this a "sidebar" conversation, but it could be revealing.

Hal and I worked with my long-time foundation grant writer, Kelly Hart, to raise the $300,000 needed, starting with an initial $40,000 of seed money. Friends and family did come forward with sufficient funding to produce two trailers and develop a website, but alas, COVID-19 would make further filming impossible. Kelly helped create several proposals for funding from NPR, the Catapult Film Fund, and ITVS, but we didn't have enough footage and support to get our financing.

Individual giving would trickle to nothing, and the growing political shift to the right and "MAGA" politics picturing migrants as a threatening, violent caravan complicated our efforts. Here's the response from one of my largest individual donors when I asked for additional funds to continue filming:

"If that means what I think it means (other countries suck, so their people are desperate for something better, and their governments don't want to pay to take care of their criminals, so they all head to the USA and cross our borders illegally and somehow, we've failed them) I wouldn't be interested in it on any level."

The growing bi-partisan politics in the U.S., where hate talk and misinformation are the norms, currently make migration reform difficult. After closing the production down, I miss the almost daily interaction with Hal. We constantly discussed the latest news from Guatemala and immigration/border advocacy and human rights organizations like the Guatemala Human Rights Commission. Hal was a PCV in Bolivia and had a "mixed marriage" - his wife is Hungarian, and Budapest was his second city.

Many friends and colleagues helped raise funds and awareness as we developed our documentary. Many professionals worked pro-bono, like Hal and me, and the rest worked for a reduced rate. Hal established a partnership with the Wisconsin Arts Foundation at the University of Wisconsin so people could send gifts through them and obtain a tax credit. Several of my high school friends from Evergreen, Dave, and Patty, sent checks in. Our philanthropic leader was Ross Freezer, a returned Peace Corps volunteer in the Dominican Republic, where he met his wife. Ross and I were board members of Partnering for Peace. Ross underwrote Hal's production of several promotional videos, including one in the Dominican Republic providing textbooks to local schools and libraries, which Rotarians sent. Ross supported the program and Hal's filming and was interested in helping fund our documentary's initial costs. As a successful entrepreneur, he had the desire to serve as well as the means to provide some severe funding, which is a powerful combination.

We fought the good fight and still have much to do to help others appreciate the potential and challenges of making changes in Guatemala and U.S. immigration policies so that so many don't have to flee to the North. And I know we'll continue to learn, analyze, and look for opportunities to help Guatemalans who need our advocacy, understanding, and support.

Guatemalan writer Francisco Goldman also became a key to our plans as his book, **The Art of Political Murder**, gained recognition through the HBO production of it and won the award for best documentary. His knowledge of Guatemala's internal politics, violence, and corruption made him a logical candidate.

I've stayed in touch with Francisco about several matters, including protests against the jailing of editor/publicist José Rubén Zamora. I reported his unjustified incarceration to PEN America, a global network of writers and publishers promoting freedom of expression, which immediately joined other human rights freedom of expression advocates in condemning the detention for no other reason than reporting on the central government's corruption. Francisco wrote a timely article about incarceration in the *New York Times* and, on YouTube, read from *The Satanic Verses* in protest of the brutal stabbing of Salman Rushdie during a presentation in New York.

Lessons Learned (final thoughts on the attempt to produce a documentary)

Once we began researching our documentary, we became aware that many of the issues of racism and challenges of the Maya community had already been filmed. Luis Argueta's work about the plight of immigrants was considerable. Skylight producer/co-founder Pamela Yates produced *When the Mountains Tremble* to *Granito* and *500 Years*. Skylight amplified stories of resistance and resilience of the majority of the Indigenous Maya population.

These compelling documentaries motivated us to double down on identifying Maya leaders to tell the broader story.

We decided to include Francisco Goldman, among others, to represent the backdrop of the growing political violence and corruption in Guatemala.

But interacting with professionals with differing political persuasions became a challenge for reasons articulated by Elizabeth Burgos, co-author of one of Rigoberta Menchú's books as told by David Stoll in ***The Battle of Rigoberta***:

> *...the critics have mixed their scholarly calling with their political beliefs, converting oral literature - the most supple of genres and the most subject to personal invention - into an almost religious canon, bordering on the absolute...*

I was taken aback by the dissent and frequent hostility between professionals who helped us with the documentary. One filmmaker disassociated themselves from us because we took advice from North American anthropologist David Stoll, who wrote ***Between Two Armies in the Ixil Towns of Guatemala*** on how the Ixil Mayas were caught between the violence of the army and the guerrilla movement - neither of which represented their better interests.

This analysis incensed some left-leaning intellectuals who promoted the notion that the Mayas became ideological revolutionaries due to centuries of exploitation. Stoll got into additional hot water when he questioned the authenticity of Maya Peace Prize Laureate Rigoberta Menchú's book, ***My Name is Rigoberta Menchú,*** about her conscientious political growth, as it was co-written with fellow socialist Elizabeth Burgos, who was married to Regis Debray, a Marxist French intellectual associated with the Marxist revolutionary, Che Guevara.

Arturo Arias presented the polemic in ***The Rigoberta Menchú Controversy,*** including a response by David Stoll. Stoll identified yet another power block in Guatemala, the Evangelical Christians, when he wrote, *Is Latin America Turn-*

*ing Protestant?,*which showed how Maya communities were also caught between the interests of the Catholic and Evangelical congregations, ignoring much of the Maya belief system. But to a degree, neither camp would ever see eye to eye and preferred not to have anything to do with one another.

I was aware of another academic controversy since anthropologist Richard Adams was one of my professors at the Institute of Latin American Studies. His magnum opus was **Crucifixion by Power***,*which veered from the traditional community-based focus toward broader national and global structures. One faction of the leftist intellectual community denounced "adamcismo" as exemplifying an era of "anthropology of occupation." Despite his critics, Adams became a tireless student of Guatemala and, with his wife Betty, became an ex-pat with houses in Austin and Panjalachel. Their oldest daughter, Tani, followed in her father's footsteps and researched and wrote about social and political challenges.

As I remember, I did very poorly in Adams' class. I opted to work with Marxist theoretician and economist Harry Cleaver at the Institute of Latin American Studies at the University of Texas in Austin. My thesis was "An Analysis of the Class Struggle from a Working-class Perspective: Example Guatemala."

Although the study helped me appreciate some of the historical and underlying causes of the poverty and lack of control of the land of the Maya communities, it did little to appreciate the implications of the considerable differences between Maya communities and how local beliefs and traditions needed to be considered. Often, the Maya and the rural poor are treated as a homogeneous group exploited for their cheap labor, which explains many of the ills in Guatemala. Consequently, I've found that much of the socialist curriculum at the university level leads to much rhetoric and frustration without providing viable economic and social programs, which lead to possible solutions to the problems of the country's most neglected population.

Rigoberta Menchú wrote a revealing article in **Travelers' Tales: Central America, True Stories** on a pilgrimage to her hometown of Laj Chimel in the Ixil Triangle region, which reflected some of the complexity in rural Guatemala and why the explanation of violence in the highlands goes beyond the commentary of these competing ideologies. According to Menchú:

> *There had been so much violence, death, and disintegration within the armed struggle. No one ever knew who killed whom or what had happened where. It is a place which holds many mysteries, secret graves, people eaten by animals...*
>
> *Everyone took justice into their own hands. Some people used it to act against their neighbors because of land. Or women, or jealousy, and for all kinds of problems. Three or four communities had title to the same piece of land.... Many landowners' sons became assassins, killing in broad daylight...."*

This social and economic complexity was a good reason to interview community leaders and members who lived with the economic and cultural challenges daily for our documentary, not just the "experts." The inability to agree on anything and criticize anyone, not just someone of a particular ideological persuasion, was unfortunate because members of the ruling elite are laser-focused on maintaining their control of society.

The four years of developing our documentary were revealing and opened the doors to meet and work with some fantastic, animate leaders and visionaries on the state of life in Guatemala. Looking back, I'm proud we learned so much, but also aware of how much we don't know or fully understand and the importance of exploring new avenues to share the underlying causes of immigration and viable solutions on the Guatemala and U.S. levels.

Epilogue

The production process was a revealing journey. We learned a lot and made many friends along the way. We fought the good fight and still have much to do to help others appreciate the potential and challenges of making changes in Guatemala and U.S. immigration policies so that so many don't have to flee to the North.

PART IV

CONTEMPORARY GUATEMALA

Chapter 17

DEMOCRACY IN CRISIS

Multiple children's caskets in the highlands. (Guatemalan Civil War. (2023, October 31 Wikipedia)

Guatemala is best known for its volcanic landscapes, Maya culture, the colorful colonial city of Antigua, a UNESCO World Heritage Site, and the picturesque Lake Atitlán, surrounded by volcanos. And yet, the spectacular setting and fascinating culture can't cover up the underlying brutality due to the greed and racism of the corrupt business and government elite. Nor can I, as a North American, ignore my country's role in creating this sad reality.

The August 2022 issue of *The Economist* revealed that although the economy had grown steadily, "...roughly half of Guatemalans, many of them Indigenous, live on less than $5.50 a day (adjusted for local purchasing power), and the country has the world's fourth highest incidence of child malnutrition. Its biggest export is people: the 1.5 million Guatemalans who live in the United States sent back remittances equal to 15% of the GDP in 2020."

Exporting cheap labor to the United States has become the principal industry of Guatemala, among other Central American countries. According to anthropologist David Stoll, in 2018, Guatemala, El Salvador, and Honduras received $19.5 billion in remittances, mainly from the U.S., and received a total of $20 billion from all their other exports combined, making the exportation of labor to the U.S. their principal industry.

And here lies the dilemma: Guatemala's government is not willing to stop the flow of their population to endure the dangers of passing through Mexico and crossing the border into the U.S. These remittances are distributed unequally, creating competition for resources where some families benefit, and others are forced to enter into a system of human trafficking to survive.

David Stoll traces the impact of remittances on one community in the highlands of Guatemala, Nebaj, highlighting how remittances have inflated the price of land to the point that locals can't afford to buy it. In *El Norte or Bust*, the author tells how migrants and their families are losing the land and homes they pledged as collateral. The growth of migration, moneylending, and large families have turned into pyramid schemes in which people experiencing poverty are forced to transfer risk and loss to those closest to them.

Despite the negative impact of the United Fruit Company's efforts to clear much of Guatemala's land for their bananas in the 1950s, significant corporations continued to control essential resources and displace Maya farmers to increase their profits, all with the support of the Guatemalan government. According to another recent report from NA-CLA, Maya communities demanding to be consulted about foreign-owned nickel mines in their territory now live under a state of siege.

Guatemala's president, Alejandro Giammattei, declared a state of siege (martial law) in El Estor, Izabal, in response to clashes between Indigenous Q'eqchi land defenders and the state police. The Indigenous community is protecting their land from toxic waste damage impacting local fishermen and farmers.

A Swiss chemical company, Solvay, operates the Fénix Nickel Mine. In 1965, the military government handed mining giant EXMIBAL a forty-year lease on 385 square kilometers in Q'eqchi territory, which involved the forced removal of Indigenous communities and supporting extractive industries as part of a national economic development model. According to Cultural Survival, a not-for-profit group protecting Indigenous rights, hundreds of members of the National Civil Police and Army raided the community radio station in El Estor.

Increasingly, Guatemalans are forced to pay import prices for food that was once grown domestically. According to a NACLA report, On April 26 and 27, 2022, Guatemalans demonstrated throughout the country, blocking roads and demanding an end to high food and fuel prices, as well as calling for government accountability and the resignation of President Alejandro Giammattei.

One participant said, "It is about more than land to harvest. It is about the people who inhabit it and, above all, the natural resources, which is what the Indigenous communities in Guatemala protect."

The report says that "the current government is striving to expand its export commodities, such as sugarcane and African palm oil." President Giammattei claims that the crops are vital to reducing poverty. However, for Indigenous Guatemalans, large agricultural businesses create food insecurity. Monoculture plantations occupy "much of the country's most cultivable land, meaning there is little opportunity for *campesinos* to practice *milpa,* a self-sustaining agricultural practice that Indigenous Mayas have historically used."

The Comité de Desarrollo Campesino (Campesino Development Committee, CODECA) was instrumental in organizing the protests demanding that the Guatemalan government give voice and recognition to the country's Indigenous nations. A critical trend for the future is that CODECA has been gaining support beyond its typical Indigenous and Campesino base, achieving an ideological following from urban communities, students, and even the middle class.

Politically, the existing president, Mr. Giammattei, is one of the least popular presidents in Latin America. Only six of one hundred and nine congressmen in Guatemala are Maya, though they still represent over 50% of the population. The corruption and influence of drug cartels have forced the country to the brink of becoming a failed state.

According to the North American Congress on Latin America (NACLA) report in January 2022, "25 Years After the Peace Accords, Democracy Weak in Guatemala:"

> *Guatemala is experiencing a weakening of democratic structures and the further entrenchment of corruption and impunity. The country is plunging into other violence and civil strife, contributing to thousands' forced displacement and migration. Some of the root causes of the war, such as land and structural inequalities and the marginalization and exploitation of Indigenous peoples continue. Despite this, Indigenous and oppressed peoples in Guatemala continue to struggle to build a democratic and dignified future.*

The credibility of the upcoming presidential elections was threatened when Guatemala's Supreme Electoral Tribunal rejected the candidacies of Indigenous leader Thelma Cabrera and her vice-president, Jordán Rodas, according to Human Rights Watch and the Washington Office on Latin America (WOLA). Cabrera received more votes in the last presidential elections than any Maya candidate (10%), which includes Nobel Peace Prize recipient Rigoberta Menchú. Rodas is the country's previous ombudsperson who was in charge of investigating corruption. He joins over twenty judges, lawyers, and magistrates forced to leave the country by the existing administration.

In early March 2023, Cabrera and Rodas were interviewed on *Democracy Now*, which revealed that not only was the Maya Mam Human Rights Environmental advocate, Cabrera, banned from participation, but that the daughter of former President Efraim Rios Montt, Zuri Montt's candidacy had been accepted. Rios Montt was convicted of the genocide of the Maya people, adding insult to past injuries to the Maya community.

Cabrera and Rodas represent the leftist Movement for the Liberation of People, which emerged from CODECA, an Indigenous-led farmers' rights organization. Both referred to the impact of the "Pact of the Corrupt," representing an alliance of the key political and economic sectors promoting the status quo. Their goal is not to promote their candidacy as much as to promote a people's famous "Constitutional Convention," resulting in an accurate representation of the Maya community, not just symbolic participation, and whose mandate would be to focus on structural changes necessary to fight the growing corruption in the country.

Despite these anomalies, the election continued, and election officials rejected an attempt by the ruling business and political elite to overturn the results of the first round of the presidential election. Sandra Torres, the former first lady accused of corruption, and her allies challenged the results of June's first-round elections, which saw the progressive, anti-corruption candidate, Bernardo Arévalo, win second place and force a runoff.

An electoral court said the final results of the first round had stayed the same after the review. Protests erupted in Guatemala City after the review suspended the certification of election results. "It was really difficult for us to compete in this election, and now they are saying we manipulated the results," says Samuel Pérez Álvarez, a Guatemalan congress member who leads the progressive political party Movimiento Semilla. "This regime is not only corrupt but authoritarian." The runoff election was held in August 2023 between Torres and Arévalo, which, surprisingly, Arévalo won.

The irony of this process is that initially, the sixty-four-year-old Bernardo Arévalo was not even considered a viable candidate, but he came in second with 12% of the votes. And he is the son of the first democratically elected President of Guatemala, whom the CIA overthrew with a financed coup in 1954. Arévalo said his unexpected second-place finish and the many blank and spoiled ballots indicated an overwhelming widespread rejection of Guatemala's corrupt status quo.

These abuses are possible, at least in part, due to a lack of transparency and accountability, as was the case, José Rubén Zamora. According to Liesl Gerntholtz, director of the PEN/Barbey Freedom to Write Center at PEN America,

> *The arrest of José Rubén Zamora is politically motivated and an egregious effort to undermine press freedom, as well as an unconscionable attempt by the Guatemalan government to silence journalists through intimidation. The Guatemalan government should immediately release Zamora and drop all charges against him.*

Not surprisingly, The World Justice Project's "rule of law index" ranks Guatemala 110 out of 140 countries worldwide. As long as these conditions and injustices continue, Guatemalans will be forced to flee their land and continue to head north for a better way of life - just another reason why we should care.

The Role of the Writer

Miguel Angel Asturias used his knowledge of the Maya to share their traditions with millions through his writing. Victor Montejo returned to his community in the highlands of Guatemala and continues to research and share the struggles and successes of the Indigenous community through his prolific writing and teaching.

More than forty thousand Guatemalans were deported by bus from the U.S. last year, making this an ongoing, unnatural disaster worthy of our best minds and talents to find viable solutions. I've written extensively on Guatemala over the years and hoped to expand my audience by producing a documentary, *Trouble in the Highlands*, dealing with many of the issues raised in my writing.

I've always tried to identify and support the local leaders and community efforts that are meeting the needs of Indigenous communities while strengthening their culture. Although the production of the documentary didn't prosper, this book will hopefully inspire more people to learn about Guatemala and Central America and support the organizations and leaders willing to move the country forward in benefiting most of its inhabitants.

Chapter 18

POSTSCRIPT: REFLECTIONS OF A LIFE WELL TRAVELED

I USED TO WONDER WHAT I WOULD BECOME WHEN I GREW UP. THEN, ABOUT SEVEN YEARS AGO, I REALIZED THAT I NEVER WAS GOING TO GROW UP—THAT GROWING IS AN EVER-ONGOING PROCESS. M. SCOTT PECK, FURTHER ALONG THE ROAD LESS TRAVELED

Fifty years of traveling the world and learning about different countries and cultures, often among the most remote, poor areas of the world, forced me to witness untold poverty, injustice, incredible resilience, determination, and bravery. This transformational experience led me to share some of my stories and work with other like-minded people to learn more about the underlying causes of such extensive poverty and appreciate the strengths and resources other countries represent, which can lead to meaningful change and improved quality of life.

So, I embarked on what was a new career. I found writing challenging, and the publishing industry has changed at a dizzying speed over the years. I was fortunate to connect with the Peace Corps Writers Group, Peace Corps Worldwide, to publish my first book, **Different Latitudes.** Fellow Returned Peace Corps writers were willing to point me in the right direction and offer their input on writing something worth reading and possibly impacting others to show empathy for those in need worldwide.

My second book, **My Saddest Pleasures: 50 Years on the Road,** would become part of my "Yin & Yang of Travel." Paul Theroux referred to this as "Travel is the saddest of pleasures. It gave me eyes." This idea became the basis for one of my favorite books, ***My Saddest Pleasure***, by Moritz Thomsen, who wrote the iconic Peace Corps experience book, ***Living Poor***. Two stories occurred in Guatemala, and a publishing house in India, Cyberwit.net, would produce the book.

Life is an ongoing learning process, and I am an avid reader. I've learned so much from fellow writers, so reviewing books was my natural vocation. I've reviewed over eighty books and set aside at least an hour to read journals and books daily.

Reviewing books is an excellent excuse to read and analyze my learning. It also allows me to connect with, and sometimes befriend, fellow writers who always need more reviews and exposure for their work. The stories I read and learned from provide considerable material to write essays published in literary journals, thus expanding my writing world and connecting me to even more writers and readers. This book includes those focused on my second country, Guatemala.

Some of those stories provide a platform to share my concerns about social injustice and inequality, like a recent essay on race, "The Souls of Black Folk: Why Some of Us Have So Much Trouble Talking About Race." This essay allowed me to share works of Black and Queer authors whose work is often ignored or banned, and I wrote it during Black History Month.

A desire to identify injustices and offer different perspectives leading to real solutions resulted in my monthly newsletter, *The Million Mile Walker Dispatch*. It provides an ideal opportunity to share my global worldview and opine about what's happening around me. "Culture Watch," one of the key segments, is a perfect place to lay out some of the fundamental challenges facing us and share alternative perspectives and, where possible, tangible solutions to our society's challenges today.

As a board member of Advance Guatemala and Partnering for Peace, I promoted partnerships and access resources for organizations making a real difference in Guatemala and worldwide. By joining PEN America, I was connected to fellow writers worldwide, promoting freedom of expression and countering the growing movement to ban books and rewrite history in favor of a powerful few.

Having more time to be a good friend, husband, father, and grandfather once I stepped back from fundraising work supporting several international development agencies has been most rewarding. Working out of my home for the last seven years has allowed me to spend more time with my three children (all born in Guatemala) and eight grandkids - and they all live within forty-five minutes of us.

Several years ago, my wife, Ligia, and I traveled to Guatemala with two of our children and their spouses. We spent time in Antigua, around Lake Atitlán, and Chichicaste-nango outside the church, climbing up to the Maya area with its traditional ceremonies. Now, we're thinking about future visits with our grandkids to introduce them to the Land of the Eternal Spring and allow them to improve their Spanish.

We plan to enroll some of the grandkids in a Spanish school in Antigua and then head up to San Jerónimo in Baja Verapaz to spend time with some of my wife's cousins and family members. And they'll have many other cousins to get to know in Guatemala City. Facebook has helped us all stay in touch with our Guatemalan friends and family, but personal contact and relationship building make for ongoing connec-tions and appreciation of Guatemala.

I plan to move ahead with my next book, ***The Moritz Thomsen Reader*** which was inspired by the two writers who knew him best and admired him the most, Tom Miller (***Panama Hat Trail***) and Paul Theroux (***Mosquito Coast***).

Fellow writers like Tom Miller and Francisco Goldman are an inspiration to work with and, through PEN America, are promoting freedom of the press and responding to violence against writers in countries like Guatemala.

Thanks to Avex Cojit, I know the outstanding work of Cultural Survival, which is instrumental in protecting Indigenous rights and promoting local leadership to solve problems impacting the Maya communities. The Guatemalan Human Rights Association is another important source of information and advocacy in favor of leadership promoting positive change in the country.

I have an unlimited amount of stories to share. Becoming a writer has introduced me to a new group of creative, caring people; many are in, or connected to, my second home and country, Guatemala. I invite my readers to pick up one of my other books and those in the bibliography to learn something new about the beautiful place. Visit with your church mission or NGO group, or pick up a tour and explore. Above all, support the local organizations that are ringing the clarion bell about corruption and injustice, vote for politicians here in the U.S. who have the needs of immigrants at heart, and welcome and support those who do make it here successfully.

Bibliography/Resources

Essays by Mark D. Walker, Which Appear in This Book

The Making of "In the Kingdom of Mescal: An Indian Fairy Tale for Adults,"*Revue Magazine*, April 2018 issue.

Maya Gods & Monsters: Supernatural Stories from the Underworld and Beyond, *Revue Magazine*, April 2019 Issue.

"Hugs not Walls: Reuniting the Children," by Mark D. Walker, *Arizona Literary Magazine 2020*, November 2019. It was reissued in *Revue Magazine*, December Edition, *2019*.

"Trouble in the Highlands," by Mark D. Walker, *WorldView Magazine*, Summer Issue, 2019, Reissued in *Revue Magazine*, September 2019.

"Justice & Responsibility: The Plight of the Immigrants from Central America," by Mark D. Walker, *Quail Bell*, July 2019.

"Land Conflicts Targeting Indigenous Communities Intensify in Northern Guatemala," by Rich Brown, NACLA, December 19, 2022.

"Time Among the Maya: Travels in Belize, Guatemala, and Mexico - Personal Reflections," *Revue Magazine*, April Issue, 2022.

"Victor Montejo's Dream for a Secure Maya Community," *Revue Magazine*, October issue, 2020.

"**Allegro to Guatemala: An Expatriate Journey Through the Land Of the Eternal Spring,**"*Revue Magazine*, June 2022.

"**Uncovering the Art of Francisco Goldman,**" *Revue Magazine*, October issue, 2021.

"**Traveling Through the Land of the Eternal Spring: A Literary Journey,**" *Literary Traveler*, April 27, 2022.

"**My Life in the Land of the Eternal Spring: The Coffee Plantation,**"*Ragazine*, July 2018.

"**My Saddest Pleasures: First Stop Guatemala,**" *Revue Magazine*, May 2022.

"**Traveling in Tandem with a Chapina,**"*Revue Magazine*, August 2019.

"**Tschiffely's Epic Ride,**"*Literary Traveler*, February 2021.

"**The Future of the Peace Corps in Guatemala,**"*Revue Magazine*, February issue, 2021.

"**Hugs not Walls: Reuniting the Children,**"*Revue Magazine*, December 2019.

"**Justice & Responsibility: The Plight of the Immigrants from Central America,**"*Quail Bell*, July 2019.

"**Crossing Borders, Building Bridges: A Journalist Heart in Guatemala,**" *Revue Magazine*, July Issue, 2021.

Trouble in the Highlands: A Documentary Film Production, *Revue Magazine*, September 2019.

THE GUATEMALA FACT SHEET

	1970	2023
Population	4,750,000 ('68)	17,980,803
Indigena	43.3% ('64)	41.7%
Ladino	56.7% ('64)	56%
Infant Mortality Rate	19.8 deaths/1000 live births	25.57 deaths/1000 live births
Life Expectancy	52.15* years	73.18 years
Literacy	30-40%	83.3%
Education Life Expectancy	0.2 years**	11 years
% Urban	35.55%	53.1%

Religious Affiliation		
Catholic	95%	41.7%
Evangelical	5%	38.8%
Internally Displaced Peoples		242,000
Guatemalans in the U.S.	118,000	1.8 million
Foreign Corporate Investment	0.03 Billion	200 US Firms, 22.5 Billion

This information was obtained through the CIA World Fact Book unless otherwise indicated by:

* **MacroTrends:** a research platform that enables users to screen and research stocks, commodities, precious metals, oil, gas, and global metrics. Seattle, Washington, United States. www.macrotrends.net.

****Knoema Corporation** is a privately owned New York Technology company.

I went back to 1970 to provide a fifty-year spread because this is what life was like when I arrived in Guatemala in 1971. The number of Guatemalans has increased noticeably, giving it one of Latin America's highest population increase rates. The percentage of the Indigena/Maya population has remained steady, and religious affiliation went from 95% Catholic in 1970 to almost 40% Evangelicals today. The number of Guatemalans in the U.S. has increased markedly, as has the level of Foreign Direct Investment, especially from the U.S.

A Comparative Chart Based on the Atlas of Impunity

	Guatemala	Honduras	Nicaragua	Bolivia	U.S.
Impunity Overall	40	84	38	75	118
Conflict/Violence	27	84	38	75	18
Environmental Degradation	14	84	92	91	33
Unaccountable/ Governance	47	42	14	73	140
Abuse/Human Rights	78	70	36	86	96
Economic Exploitation	38	43	36	58	123

Published by the Eurasia Group and the Chicago Council on Global Affairs, this chart scores all 197 countries and territories across five areas of impunity: abuse of human rights, unaccountable governance, conflict and violence, economic exploitation, and environmental degradation. All involve the abuse of power. Atlas uses more than 65 independent, credible, and comparable data sources to produce a score for each country.

The lower the numbers, the worse the condition. Afghanistan is the worst, Finland is the best, Guatemala is on par with Nicaragua, and the U.S. is in the middle. Guatemala is the fourteenth worst in the world for environmental degradation, which reflects the impact of climate change and could mean the death knell for the habitat of the national bird, the Quetzal. Guatemala has a lower score than Honduras for conflict/violence and is close to Nicaragua in economic exploitation.

GUATEMALA DOCUMENTARY RESOURCE LIST

Recommended Books

Different Latitudes: My Life in the Peace Corps and Beyond, by Mark D. Walker, Peace Corps Worldwide, 2017.

My Saddest Pleasures: 50 Years on the Road, Part of the Yin and Yang of Travel Series, by Mark D. Walker, Cyberrwit.net, 2022.

The Guatemala Reader: History, Culture, Politics (The Latin America Readers) by Greg Grandin, Deborah T. Levenson, et al. Duke University Press 2011.

The Brothers: John Foster Dulles, Allen Dulles, and Their Secret World War, by Stephen Kinzer, Times Books, New York 2013.

Love in a Fearful Land, by Henri J.M Nouwen, Orbis Books, Maryknoll, New York 2006.

Silence on the Mountain: Stories of Terror, Betrayal, and Forgetting in Guatemala, by Daniel Wilkinson, Duke University Press 2004.

The Art of Political Murder: Who Killed the Bishop?, by Francisco Goldman, Grove Press, New York 2007.

Monkey Boy, by Francisco Goldman, Grove Press, New York 2021.

The Line Becomes a River: Dispatches from the Border, by Francisco Cantu, Riverhead Books, New York 2018.

Bitter Fruit: The Story of the American Coup in Guatemala, Revised and Expanded (Series on Latin American Studies), by Stephen Schlesinger et al. David Rockefeller Center for Latin American Studies; 2nd edition, 2005.

Maya Intellectual Renaissance, by Victor Montejo, the University of Texas Press, Austin 2005.

Entre Dos Mundos, by Victor Montejo, Piedrasanta, Guatemala 2021.

The Adventures of Mr. Puttison Among the Maya, by Victor Montejo, YAX TE' Foundation 2002.

Voices From Exile, by Victor Montejo, University of Oklahoma Press, Norman, 1999.

Me Llamo Rigoberta Menchú y Así Me Nació la Conciencia, by Elizabeth Burgos, Siglo Veintiuno Editores, SA, 1985.

Between Two Armies In The Ixil towns of Guatemala, by David Stoll, Columbia University Press, New York 1993.

Rigoberta Menchú and the Story of All Poor Guatemalans, by David Stoll, Westview, 1999.

El Norte or Bust!: How Migration Fever and Microcredit Produced a Financial Crash in a Latin American Town, byDavid Stoll,Rowman & Littlefield Publishers; 1st edition 2012.

Guatemalan Indians and the State 1540 to 1988, by Carol Smith ed. With the assistance of Marilyn M. Moors, Austin: University of Texas Press 1990.

Sons of the Shaking Earth, by Eric Wolf, Chicago University of Chicago Press, 1959.

Penny Capitalism: A Guatemalan Indian Economy, by Sol Tax, Washington Institute of Social Anthropology, Smithsonian Institution 1953.

Historia del Café de Guatemala, by Regina Wagner, Villegas Editores 2001.

Guatemala, by Susanne Jonas and David Tobis, North American Congress on Latin America 1981.

Guatemala: The Politics of Land Ownership, by Thomas and Marjorie Melville, Free Press, New York 1972.

Through a Glass Darkly, The US Holocaust in Central America, by Thomas R. Melville, Xlibris Corporation, Philadelphia, 2005.

Guatemala: Unnatural Disaster, by Roger Plant, Latin American Bureau, London, 1978.

The Harvest of Violence: The Guatemalan Indian and the Guatemalan Crisis, by Robert Carmack, ed. University of Oklahoma Press, Norman 1988.

Massacres in the Jungle: Ixcán, Guatemala 1975-1982, by Ricardo Falla, Translated by Julia Howland, Westview Press, Boulder 1994.

Confessions of an Economic Hitman, by John Perkins, Plume 2005.

Guatemalan Journey, by Stephen Connely Benz, University of Texas Press, Austin 1996.

The Volcanoes Above Us, by Norman Lewis, Penguin Books, 1957.

Central America's Forgotten History: Revolution, Violence, and the Roots of Migration, by Aviva Chomsky, Beacon Press, 2021.

How Can I Make A Difference?

Are you looking for ways to make a real difference in the lives of Guatemalans and help preserve their vibrant cultural heritage? You can help by becoming informed about Guatemala's challenges and actively participating in efforts to influence your sphere of influence about Guatemala and the needs of immigrants. **The Guatemala Reader** offers an extensive bibliography of fiction and nonfiction books, serving as an excellent starting point and a valuable resource to deepen your understanding of Guatemala's history and challenges.

Additionally, you can support the remarkable leaders, advocates, and artists featured in the book, as well as the organizations dedicated to directly improving the quality of life for Guatemalans through sustainable development initiatives. Having personally worked with and gotten to know these organizations, I can confidently recommend their effectiveness.

Advance Guatemala

Guatemalan-American entrepreneur **J.P. Dahdah, CEO of Vantage Self-Directed Retirement Plans**, founded **Advance Guatemala**. When I met J.P., we realized we had a shared vision for helping local organizations make a difference in education, health, small business development, and housing. As a founding Board member, I helped identify partners, including the Wheelchair Foundation, Project CURE, Hug It Forward, and Namaste Direct. J.P. takes donors to see the work first-hand to engage donors and establish ongoing partnerships with some of Guatemala's most at-risk communities.

Advance Guatemala has provided much-appreciated support for making this book so it can reach a wider audience eager to explore the complexities and possibilities within Guatemala. For more information on **Advance Guatemala** and their impactful initiatives, please visit their website: https://advanceguatemala.org/who-we-are/

Namaste Direct

Founder Bob Graham arrived in Guatemala about the same time I did as a Kellogg Foundation Fellow. He's a social entrepreneur and initially set up the Katalysis Partnership to promote microenterprises. He also set up Namaste Direct, with an unwavering focus on economically empowering Guatemalan women to achieve financial security.

I received funding from them for some projects with World Neighbors and introduced him to J.P. Dahdah, and Advance Guatemala supported a Namaste Direct program in Guatemala. Bob's memoir, *50-50-at 50*, inspired me to write *Different Latitudes: My Life in the Peace Corps and Beyond.* We've shared our love of Guatemala for over 30 years. You can find out more at https://namastedirect.org/about-us/

Seeds for a Future

Seeds for a Future aims to foster rural community development that integrates permaculture, nutrition education, and micro-business opportunities. Based on the coaching and mentoring of families to provide the skills and materials they need for success, the Seeds self-reliance model also fosters the development of "home-grown" leadership, facilitating the program's spread throughout the community.

In 2004, founders Suzanne and Earl de Berge volunteered at a Pre-Classic Maya archaeology site beneath the village of Chocolá. Joined by other archaeology volunteers, they formed Seeds for a Future, a U.S. non-profit in 2007 that has helped over 2,400 families in 19 communities on the South Coast.

I met with Suzanne and Earl several years ago to discuss fundraising initiatives, which is when I learned about their commitment to Guatemala and that Earl was a poet and author. We've worked together ever since, including my essay in this book about ex-patriates in Guatemala. You can find out more at <u>https://seedsforafuture.org/purpose/</u>

Cultural Survival

They've been advocating for Indigenous Peoples' rights and supporting Indigenous communities' self-determination, cultures, and political resilience since 1972. I met their Program Director, Avexim Cojti (Maya K'iche'), Director of Programs. Both Avex and her father, Demetrio, a professor and author in his own right, provided invaluable insights on the plight of the Maya community for the documentary I was working on, **Trouble in the Highlands.**

Our focus was programs and projects that supported Indigenous communities' self-determination and rights, especially in Community Media and Indigenous Radio programs. She knew and worked with another of my "Extraordinary Lives," Maria Martin, and her media training center, Gracias Vida. Qualified journalists and leadership are critical to the development and growth of the Maya community. You can learn more about them at <u>https://www.culturalsurvival.org/about</u>.

Acknowledgments

For suggestions, improvements, and encouragement for my opus on Guatemala, I'd like to thank my primary editors, Bill Harbrick and Susan Pohlman. Fellow Returned Peace Corps Volunteer and prolific writer Lawrence F. Lihsosit has been a constant help and inspiration. Other invaluable supporters include Luis Argueta, Hal Rifken, Chati Cajas, Ken Ekstrom, John Timm, David Carlson, Sue Patterson, Cliff Nagel, Paul and Ruth Hickey, Bob Scully, Buck Denies, Ross Feezer, Mark Schneider, David Stoll, and Carol Karasik, as well as Earl and Susanne de Berg.

My special thanks to Terry and John Korick Biskovich, the editors of the English language publication *Revue Magazine* where I was a contributing writer. They've highlighted the best articles, photos, and cultural materials for over thirty-one years. This digital interactive magazine has published all my essays on Guatemala and even included the video/interview from *Global Connections TV* in their February 2023 issue. Their audience includes ex-pats and bilingual readers from throughout Central America.

A shout out to the Founder of Advance Guatemala, J.P. Dahdah for the opportunity to do some good in Guatemala and for supporting this project. The host of Global Connections Television, fellow Returned Peace Corps Volunteer Bill Miller, who interviewed me about the making of each of my three books.

Also, my thanks to the Guatemalans who shared their insights and knowledge of the realities of Guatemala, starting with my wife, Ligia. Also, Luis Argueta, Victor Montejo, Chati Cajas, Avex and Demetria Cojito.

A small team of beta readers and advisors includes John Timm, Lorenzo Lihosit, Paul Hickey, Bob Forbes, and my longtime proofer, Esther Niles.

Several individuals and entities have been instrumental in helping me find my voice as a writer, starting with John Coyne and Marian Haley Beil, who manage The Peace Corps Writers group, which published my first book, ***Different Latitudes, My Life in the Peace Corps and Beyond***, as well as several Returned Peace Corps Volunteers (RPCVs) such as Alana de Joseph and John Prybot, as well as several who taught me the ropes of writing, Craig Storti, Chic Dambach, Lorenzo Lihosit, and John Coyne, as well as top writers John Thorndike and DW Jefferson.

A tight-knit group of professional writers' groups and authors in Arizona have been a constant source of technical support and encouragement, beginning with Cindi Reiss, President of the Phoenix Writers Club, and members Pam Colter, former president Uta Behrens, Kixx Goldman, Ilsa Manning, Richard McMaster, and Brad Graber. Members of the Arizona Authors Association, which hosts my column, "Million Mile Walker Review: What We're Reading and Why," especially the newsletter editors Kathleen Cook, Toby Heathcote, and Jane Ruby. Also, Karen Leitner, Susan Anderson, and Marie Fanzo of the Arizona Professional Writers Group. Sherry Kesling, who headed up the Writers Connection; Susan Pohlman, the founder of the Writers Network; Meg Files of the Tucson Book Festival; and Windy Lynn Harris of Market Coaching and Creative Writers.

Outstanding writers like Nick Hunt, Craig Storti, John Thorndike and Francisco Goldman have also been a constant support and inspiration. And what would I do without the editor for this book, Eugenia Lazaris, and the editors of the other magazines I contribute to, Francis and Linda McGovern, co-founders of *Literary Traveler*, Sarah Leahy of *Wanderlust Journal*, Onkar Sharma of *Travel Yard*, and James Cox of *Midwest Bookshelf*. And the editor-in-chief of my latest book, Dr. Karunesh Kumar Agrawal at Taj Mahal Review/C yber.net, for taking an interest in my traveler's tales. Finally, for the patience and support of my wife of fifty years, Ligia Walker.

Mark D. Walker, 2023

ABOUT THE AUTHOR AND EDITOR

Mark Walker was a Peace Corps Volunteer in Guatemala and spent over forty years helping disadvantaged people in the developing world. He's worked with groups like CARE, MAP International, Food for the Hungry, and Make-A-Wish International and was the CEO of Hagar USA.

His first book, ***Different Latitudes: My Life in the Peace Corps and Beyond***, was recognized by the Arizona Literary Association. His next book was ***My Saddest Pleasures: 50 Years on the Road***, named **Best Travel Book** by the Peace Corps

Writers' Group. Two of his articles were recognized by the "Solas Literary Award, sponsored by "Traveler's Tales," and, most recently, the Bronze for **"Best Travel Writing—Adventure Travel.**" He's a contributing writer for "Revue Magazine," "The Authors Show," "The Wanderlust Journal" and "Literary Traveler." His column, **"The Million Mile Walker Review: What We're Reading and Why,**"is part of the Arizona Authors Association newsletter, "The Authors Digest."

His honors include the "Service Above Self" award from Rotary International. He's a Board member of Advance Guatemala and the Arizona Authors Association. He was profiled in the Spring 2023 issue of The Westerner Magazine of Western Colorado University, "50 Years on the Road: A Journey from Peace Corps Volunteer to Author," and was interviewed three times on **Global Connections Television**. His wife and three children were born in Guatemala.

If you liked this book, please rate it on Amazon, Goodreads or any other platform you use to identify the books you read. You can read more of the author's work, including articles and book reviews, interviews, webinars and a gallery of photos at MillionMileWalker.com or contact him at Mar k@MillionMileWalker.com

www.ingramcontent.com/pod-product-compliance
Lightning Source LLC
Chambersburg PA
CBHW070652010826
48975CB00013B/1015